YEAR-ROUND CREATIVE THINKING ACTIVITIES for the PRIMARY CLASSROOM

Margaret C. Riley

Margaret Carol Riley has been a primary grade teacher in Virginia public schools for over ten years. Mrs. Riley earned her B.S. in Elementary Education (1979) and her M.Ed. in Administration/Supervision (1984) at George Mason University.

Donna L. Taylor

Donna L. Taylor has served in Virginia public schools as a primary classroom teacher for more than seventeen years. She earned her B.A. in History at Mary Washington College (1970) and her M.Ed. in Elementary Education at the University of Virginia (1976). Ms. Taylor has also authored a manual for instructors in the Young Readers Program, a summer reading project to promote reading among Hispanic students.

Mrs. Riley and Ms. Taylor met as resource teachers for a primary gifted education/teacher training program. They co-author and publish *Crittletivity*, an idea letter for K–5 teachers. For information regarding *Crittletivity*, write in care of the authors, Route 1, Box 299, Gainesville, VA 22065.

THE CENTER FOR APPLIED RESEARCH IN EDUCATION
West Nyack, New York 10995

Library of Congress Cataloging-in-Publication Data

Riley, Margaret C., 1956–
  Year-round creative thinking activities for the primary classroom
/ Margaret C. Riley, Donna L. Taylor.
    p. cm.
  ISBN 0-87628-985-5
  1. Creative thinking—Study and teaching. 2. Education, Primary-
Activity programs. I. Taylor, Donna L., 1948-   . II. Center for
Applied Research in Education. III. Title.
LB1590.5.R55   1990   89-49685
372.13—dc20   CIP

This book is dedicated to Dan Riley—
husband, friend, and a very creative
fellow himself.

ISBN 0-87628-985-5

THE CENTER FOR APPLIED
RESEARCH IN EDUCATION
BUSINESS & PROFESSIONAL DIVISION
A division of Simon & Schuster
West Nyack, New York 10995

Printed in the United States of America

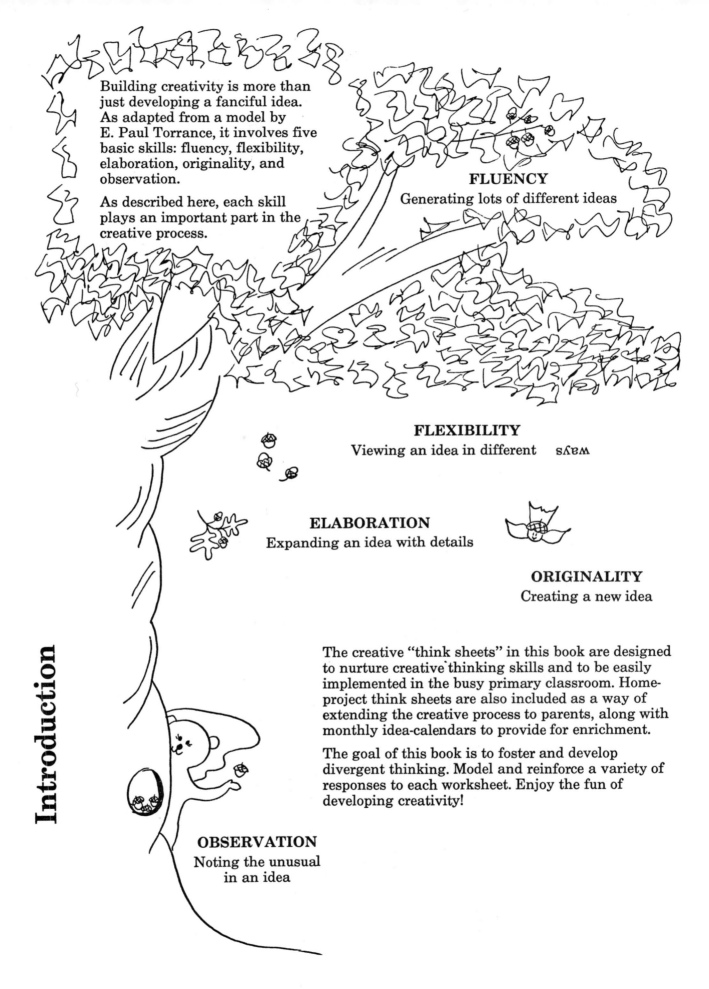

Building creativity is more than just developing a fanciful idea. As adapted from a model by E. Paul Torrance, it involves five basic skills: fluency, flexibility, elaboration, originality, and observation.

As described here, each skill plays an important part in the creative process.

FLUENCY
Generating lots of different ideas

FLEXIBILITY
Viewing an idea in different ways

ELABORATION
Expanding an idea with details

ORIGINALITY
Creating a new idea

The creative "think sheets" in this book are designed to nurture creative thinking skills and to be easily implemented in the busy primary classroom. Home-project think sheets are also included as a way of extending the creative process to parents, along with monthly idea-calendars to provide for enrichment.

The goal of this book is to foster and develop divergent thinking. Model and reinforce a variety of responses to each worksheet. Enjoy the fun of developing creativity!

OBSERVATION
Noting the unusual in an idea

Introduction

To the Teacher . . .

A variety of materials is included in this resource to help you in developing creativity. By using these materials, you will be able to:

- provide specific creative skill activities to students for each seasonal topic during the school year,
- involve parents in developing the creative process, and
- add to the classroom environment by utilizing divergent bulletin board ideas that promote creative thinking.

An ultimate goal in the creative thinking process is to promote divergent thought, which is the ability to generate a variety of possible solutions to a given problem which are all considered in the final selection of an answer or solution. Divergent thought processes can be incorporated into any assignment simply by adding questions that provide student choice or opportunities for student input. The converse, convergent thought, is a problem situation in which there is only one correct answer. Convergent activities often dominate the learning environment and center the level of thinking at the memory/comprehension level. The addition of divergent teaching activities allows children to apply knowledge and synthesize ideas. Together, divergent and convergent thought result in productive thinking. Children who work through open-ended exercises have made use of higher levels of thinking and creative problem solving.

Creative activities can be easiliy integrated into the curriculum and challenge children to use their knowledge in synthesizing ideas. All children can develop creativity by working through exercises that call for divergent thinking. As a result of using the skill sheets included in this book, the teacher will see:

- students actively involved in problem solving situations requiring divergent thought,

- activities that meet the needs of all students in the classroom . . . from the remedial to the gifted,
- learning situations that build a student's self-confidence and self-concept,
- enjoyable activities that tap into a child's natural interest in seasonal subjects,
- an opportunity to develop individual creative strengths and improve weak areas, and
- a challenged class learning how to use their creative skills to meet problem situations with a variety of possible solutions.

ABOUT THIS BOOK . . .

This book is unique in that the activities and ideas all surround Paul Torrance's idea of creativity, i.e., fluency, flexibility, originality, and elaboration. The authors, both classroom teachers, recognize a variety of difficulties that often prevent creative activities from being implemented in the primary classroom. Each of these difficulties can be overcome when considered from an alternative viewpoint. Perhaps the following thoughts will illuminate those who feel restricted in presenting creative activities . . .

The curriculum is too full already to involve creativity.

All teachers enjoy seasonal activities as part of curriculum extension throughout the year. Why not base seasonal activities on creative skill development and accomplish two goals in one?

I'm not creative . . . My students aren't creative.

Until opportunity knocks, can you be sure? When creativity is considered in the context of the skills explained on the next several pages, one can definitely reconsider! These activities are presented in an easy-access format that opens up doors to creativity.

Creative activities take too much time and often involve messy materials.

Creativity is not simply cutting and pasting a project together . . . it is an involved thinking process. Yes, the thinking process can take time. So— why not provide the time? Creative problem solving may extend over several days and be something a child engages in during spare moments or when required daily work is complete. The activities in this resource are excellent for challenging the fast worker and providing an enjoyable thinking break for the slow worker.

Margaret C. Riley
Donna L. Taylor

Contents

How to Use
Creative Thinking Activities
in Your Classroom

MANAGEMENT

INTRODUCING CHILDREN TO DIVERGENT ACTIVITIES

When students are first challenged with the types of creative activities presented in this resource, their reactions will be mixed according to their personalities. The shy child may burst into tears, the confident child will be chomping at the bit to start, the child who likes specific directions will have several questions aimed at eliciting the teacher's expectations, and the happy-go-lucky child may enjoy thinking about the activity so much that little will be put down on paper! All of these reactions are to be expected.

When first confronted with divergent activities, children need examples by which to model their own thinking and answers. Therefore, it is very important that a "warm-up" time be included for these activities. As you introduce the activities, enjoy doing them along with the class. This will alleviate the student's anxiety about what the teacher must be expecting in this new type of work! Other strategies that will help children overcome their uncertainty are to:

- Pair children and have them think together about an activity or worksheet idea by providing choices—children may use an idea the class comes up with, or think further on their own. The goal is to have them gain the confidence necessary for an independent level of thinking.

- Use a small group setting to work through the complete assignment, and then ask children to give individual responses verbally. Resist automatically expecting a written response.

Another key point to keep in mind is that there are several steps to creative thinking, whether the objective is fluency, flexibility, originality, elaboration, or observation. In each case there must be a "warm up" stage where the idea is presented and the group "plays" with the thought. Then children need time to consider their own ideas and possible responses to the worksheet/activity. Finally, after each child has decided upon the direction he/she would like to take the answer, time must be allotted for completion of the worksheet/activity. Completion time may extend further than one typical assignment period. Teachers should consider allowing carry-over to the next day for completion.

Creative thought takes time and practice. As children work through successive opportunities for divergent answers, they show greater confidence in the thinking process. It is suggested that samples of work be saved throughout the year as tangible evidence of increased variety in thought. Such documentation is also good for showing growth when conferencing with parents.

The accepting teacher who makes children feel comfortable with "weird" answers and divergent thinking will delight in the variety of responses given to any one problem. Additionally, carry-over to other curriculum tasks will surface. Children will begin to ask, "May I do this assignment this way?" rather than follow the convergent directions presented. At times, they will need to follow convergent directions. At other times, their creative alterations will enhance the work and become evidence of their confidence in using their creative abilities.

Year-Round Creative Thinking Activities for the Primary Classroom is intended to become a jumping off point for teachers. Many of the patterns can be adapted to fit other seasonal subjects. For example, within Section 1, "Back to School," there is a worksheet that extends words associated with a person's initials into creative writing. This same pattern—associating words with initials—could easily be adapted to November by using the initials for "Tom Turkey." Children can provide impetus too. Often they will enjoy a particular idea so much that they will want to repeat it in a different context. Watch for opportunities to extend the ideas presented within!

Many of the teaching suggestions included in each section are open to a variety of product possibilities. Use your creativity and that of your students to decide how to best match process and product. Once an idea is initiated, it often points its own way to a product. When the process of an activity naturally generates a product idea, exciting things happen with learning.

Possible products that children enjoy include:

book	class book
book jacket	collection
bookmark	cube
chart	debate

demonstration
diagram
diorama
discussion
drawing
filmstrip
flipbook
gameboard
graph
interview
invention
letter
list
map
mobile
model
mural
museum
painting
pamphlet
paper folding

photo essay
plan (meal, event, etc.)
poem
puppets
puzzle
rate, sequence
rebus story
report
role play
roller movie
scrap book
sculpture
shadow play
skit
song
songbook
stand-up figure
survey
timeline
writing

DEFINITIONS AND EXAMPLES OF TERMS

Each thought process may be sparked by a variety of thinking approaches. However, the *basic definitions* are:

FLUENCY—generating lots of different ideas

FLEXIBILITY—viewing an idea in different ways

ORIGINALITY—creating a new idea

ELABORATION—expanding an idea with details

OBSERVATION—noting the unusual in an idea

Consider these basic definitions in the context of "apples." A teacher might use the following activities/ideas:

FLUENCY—List lots of different kinds of apples. What are the differences?
In how many ways can apples be used?

FLEXIBILITY—How might animals use apples?
Apples are usually considered something to give to the teacher.
Why might a teacher give an apple to a student?

ORIGINALITY—What new uses for apples can you list? (Consider the attributes of apples . . . shape, size, color, texture, etc.)
Compose a story about an apple character!

ELABORATION—Design the perfect apple. Explain why it's the perfect apple!
Create a product line in which apples are the main theme, e.g., apple housewares, apple school supplies, etc.

OBSERVATION—Cut an apple in different ways. How are the pieces alike and how are they different? Use them for printing a pattern.
What different peculiarities do people and animals have in the ways they eat apples? Examples: Babies must have applesauce. Some people prefer apples without the skin.

Some of the following extended definitions may assist you in developing these thinking processes. Using one of these "stems" may help in generating answers to the preceding ideas/activities as well as those included in the remainder of this resource.

FLUENCY—brainstorming, looking for alternative solutions, listing attributes, listing possibilities, asking a variety of appropriate questions, utilizing synonyms, accepting the possibility of more than one right answer

FLEXIBILITY—using a variety of approaches to consider problems and arrive at solutions, reconsidering the viewpoint by minifying or magnifying the problem, adapting the idea to alternative situations, interpreting the information in a variety of ways

ORIGINALITY—combining the unusual, noting unusual responses, searching for unique products or ideas, reversing the question/answer process, relating unconnected information, comparing unlike objects

ELABORATION—incorporating accuracy and completeness within an idea, enhancing an answer to provide full meaning and understanding, embellishing an idea/concept/question, adding details to make a common object more interesting, filling in "gaps" in writing, stretching or extending an idea

OBSERVATION—taking a minified or magnified look at the problem/idea, considering different perspectives, comparing data, noting similarities/differences, forecasting

MANAGEMENT STRATEGIES

Use these creative skill activities as—

Morning Warm Ups . . . provide independent assignments as the children arrive	Language Arts Assignments . . . reinforce skills of writing sentences, following directions, and reading comprehension
Learning Centers . . . develop creative thinking skills in an independent way	Seasonal Extensions . . . apply academic skills through a seasonal topic
Independent Project Packets . . . challenge the fast worker	Homework Assignments . . . encourage parent-student interaction through divergent thinking
Chart Activities . . . enlarge the worksheet and use it as a basis for class or small group discussion	Parent Volunteer Activities . . . ready to use and easy to follow with individuals or small groups
Brainstorm Breaks . . . make the most of a spare moment	Supplemental Vacation Packs . . . give students challenging and entertaining free time activity ideas

CREATIVE QUESTIONING

Student response is a reflection of the questions posed by the teacher. A variety of questions enhances thinking through the levels of memory, comprehension, application, analysis, synthesis, and evaluation.

The woodland scene shown on the accompanying reproducible chart, "Woodland Wonderings," is provided as a classroom tool to help you quickly pose questions at all levels of thinking. Use the cue words when posing questions about any topic . . . just supply endings relative to specific learning objectives.

> *Example*   In a study of ANIMALS . . .
>
> If you could ADD MORE characteristics to mammals, what would they be?
>
> LIST ALL the mammals you would include in a personal zoo.

Color in the chart, laminate it, and use it as a classroom tool for both teacher and students. Students could ask for a question from the owl, the turtle, and so on. Or, students could pose an owl's question, a turtle's question, etc., for friends to answer

> Please note the thinking levels based on Torrance and Bloom's models that are associated with the animals:
>
> Owl . . . Observation, Comprehension
>
> Turtle, Bees . . . Flexibility, Synthesis
>
> Fish . . . Fluency, Synthesis
>
> Frog . . . Elaboration, Synthesis
>
> Beaver . . . Originality, Synthesis

CREATIVITY FROM A PARENT'S POINT OF VIEW

An important aspect of initiating creative activities in your classroom is giving parents an idea of what is meant by creativity and involving them in developing creative thought processes. As you communicate how creativity is integrated into your current curriculum and classroom routine, you will find that parents will become strong supporters of, and advocates for, divergent thinking opportunities. In fact, they will want ideas for home extension themselves.

To encourage parental involvement, the following pages include:

- a sample "Parent Letter" for the beginning of the year. Use this letter to let parents know about your creativity goal for the year.
- a "Creativity Criteria" sheet you can reproduce as many times as needed. Provide copies of this sheet to help parents assess whether the skill of creativity is included in commercially made games they have or would like to purchase.

Woodland Wonderings

Adapt... Rearrange...

What else? Elaborate... Add more...

Whooo... What... When... Where...

Design... Combine...

What are all...

What other ways...

How many... List all... Name all...

- a reproducible handout entitled "Posing Creative Questions at Home." This is a useful tool for Open House and for encouraging parents to extend the questioning process to the home situation.
- reproducible "Home Enrichment Calendars" for every month of the school year.

As parents become more proficient at promoting creative thinking in the home, they will find it an easy "next step" to assess their child's creativity in schoolwork. Looking at a sample of the child's writing or artwork, the parent will recognize evidence of fluency, flexibility, originality, elaboration, and observation.

This common frame of reference between parent and teacher provides a strong foundation for communication regarding student growth in creative thinking. It is hoped that the following pages will be useful in establishing that common point of reference.

Parent Letter

Dear Parents,

   Developing creative thinking skills is an important goal I have established for the students in room ___ this year. Since we are partners in the education of your child, I feel it is important that you know I will be working with a research-based model of creativity which delineates five specific components:

Fluency . . .	generating lots of different ideas
Flexibility . . .	changing gears, approaching a problem in different ways from different points of view
Originality . . .	devising unusual or unique answers
Elaboration . . .	adding details, building onto an idea
Observation . . .	noticing things others miss, comparing and contrasting data

   From time to time, I will assign home projects. These are intended to be activities which call for creative thought, involve sharing with one or more family members, and result in a product which can be shared at school.

   This month's home project is to

_____

_____

   If you have any questions, please do not hesitate to call me or write me a note.

                                   Sincerely,

                                   _____

Creativity Criteria

Skill	Definition	Game	Activity
fluency	• lots of different ideas	Does the game allow for listing, coming up with many ideas? example: word games	How many ways can you think of to display your painting?
flexibility	• change gears, approach a problem in many different ways	Are players required to take a different point of view? example: game with offensive/defensive play	Tell the story again from the point of view of a different character.
originality	• come up with unusual or unique answers	Does the game provide for player input/design? Most games aren't structured for originality, but many toys provide open-ended opportunities, i.e. blocks	Incorporate your own unique ideas into a writing or art project.
elaboration	• add details, build on an idea	Do players have a chance to add details or dramatize? example: charades, toys which require building	Create a detailed treasure map or puppet show.
observation	• notice things others miss, compare and contrast data	Does the game call for classifying or noting details? example: mazes, lotto games, dominoes, category games	Tell how book and movie versions of the same story are alike and different.

POSING CREATIVE QUESTIONS AT HOME

The easiest way to challenge children to think creatively is to ask questions that promote that kind of thinking. There are two essential keys to creative questioning:

- Make the questions open-ended so the child knows there is not just one right answer.
- Allow sufficient "wait time" for answers. Creative thinking is an involved process that often requires an "incubation period" to arrive at appropriate responses.

The following question stems are a useful tool in developing the skill of asking creative questions:

FLUENCY . . .

List all the possible . . .
How many ways . . .
What are all the uses . . .

FLEXIBILITY . . .

What different approach . . .
How else might you . . .
What other angle . . .

ORIGINALITY . . .

What unusual way . . .
No one else would think of . . .

ELABORATION . . .

What can you add to . . .
Give all the details . . .
What would give it more . . .

OBSERVATION . . .

How are they alike/different . . .
What is missing/happening/going to happen . . .
What patterns do you notice . . .

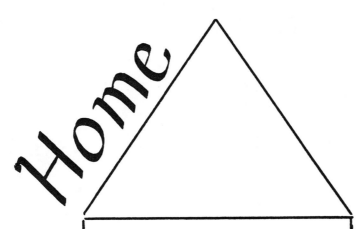

Home

Reproduce these
calendars and
send them home
regularly for
parents to use
as enrichment.

Enrichment Calendars

September

Workers Week List hard workers you know! Little Red Hen... Cinderella...	**Labor Day** Choose a career — Look in a catalog for tools, clothes appropriate to the trade.	Think of stereotyped careers...	Role play the opposite side!	Choose 3 careers — Look in the Yellow Pages for entries — Graph the number you find.	Find a fact that no one else knows about a career of your choice.	Interview someone in an interesting job! ...so say you own	Write a note to yourself about a career you'd like self. Seal it, save it, open it next Labor Day.
School Supplies Week Talk with your parents about how school supplies have changed through the years.	Survey friends for differences in school supplies.		Check your library for craft ideas to make with your school supplies.	Pretend you are a school supply item... Tell how students should take care of you!	Combine school supplies to invent a machine that would make school work easier!	Draw a poster advertising the ultimate school supply store!	Design a green kiddy organizer! school
GRAPH PAPER WEEK List all the ways people use graph paper.	Use some graph paper to map your room!	Do some number problems with graph paper.	Use two sizes of graph paper to draw the same thing.	Make a crossword puzzle using graph paper.	Color in boxes of graph paper to make letters, spell words, draw pictures!	Use graph paper to make 3-dimensional shapes!
Fall Week Make a mural about all the things that occur in fall!	List sights of fall that you enjoy most!	Listen for the most unusual fall sound you hear today.	Write a haiku (or another type of poem) about the smells of fall!	Collect "leaves"... crumble them... arrange in an artistic design!	List all the definitions of "fall" — Illustrate each one! wear a fall, fall season, fall down, waterfall	Make a list of your school favorites!
Time Capsule Week — Collect these products (and some others, if you wish) to seal in your capsule until June!	Tape an interview of your parents talking about their school days.	Make a complete list of the new things you bought for school.	Write your impressions of the first day of school.	Search for some more products of your new teacher or school.	Make a detailed map of your new classroom.	Make a list of your school favorites! ...or friend book, subject, game, hour
Decorate a shoebox. Plan where you will keep it until June.						

OCTOBER

Week							
Harvest Week Combine lots of harvest foods to make a harvest character.	Read a cookbook to find all the different things you can do with harvest foods. Try one!	Learn a harvest song or dance.	Make a mobile of things associated with harvest.	Make a harvest hat or apron using fabric crayons.	Write some harvest problems! 10 − 7 = ? were picked. ? are left!	Make − and enjoy − some pumpkin, carrot, apple, or corn muffins!
Explorers Week Make walnut shell boats. Create a finger puppet show to go with them!	Find out how big Columbus' ships were. Name some things of comparable size!	Explore some new reading material!	Explore your yard! What scientific discovery can you make?	Explore your kitchen for a utensil you've never used!	Explore a new friendship. Plan an activity with someone you'd like to know better.	Explore your neighborhood! N E W S
Pumpkins Week Find out how many different varieties of pumpkins there are!	Use pumpkin seeds to make a mosaic!	Design a scarecrow that has several pumpkin patches on it.	...grow pumpkin vines on... What other things do you know that grow on vines?	Write a picture story about a pumpkin!	Find a pumpkin recipe!	Search grocery ads... Compare pricing, marketing of pumpkins.
International Week Use the globe to define national and international areas!	Sample a new cuisine!	Make an international flag display!	Listen to some international music!	Make paper dolls and international costumes.	The ... went out to the ...	Make a word search of different countries.
Halloween Week Create a finger puppet show that involves many different characters.	Use a pulley to rig a surprise!	Draw a spider web plus a math problem in each space.	Decorate a bowl or basket for Halloween treats.	Hide some treats. Write clues for your friends to solve.	Plan your trick or treat route on a map.	Make Halloween critters from snack foods — marshmallows, pretzels, raisins,...

Learn to say "October" in different languages.

november

Election Week

- Start a week-long graph of number of newspaper articles related to elections.
- Pretend you are a candidate. Write a week of diary entries about your campaign life.
- Design that posters will remind adults to VOTE!
- Debate! What should be decided by voting... What shouldn't?
- Campaign for your favorite Friday night family activity. Does it win the family vote?
- If yes, enjoy it tonight! If not, start campaigning for next Friday!
- Use your graph from this week to write a math problem for your parents to solve!

"No" Week

- How many words can you find that have "no" in them? note nod ignore
- String your words together to make sentences.
- Make silly things you "no" which world to a list
- Say "no" with as many different inflections as you can: no, no? nooo...
- Tally how many times you hear "no" today. ||||||
- Start with no - know. Make a book of homonyms.
- Make a list (a silly one!) of all the reasons someone might not do his/her homework.

Indoor Week / Activity

- Enjoy a marathon of family games.
- List all your favorite indoor activities on a cube. Toss the cube for ideas of something to do!
- Look in forgotten nooks and crannies! House Cleaning Day!
- Research occupations related to ... categorize them by indoor/outdoor.
- Write a story "___'s Indoor Day" to share with a younger friend.
- Mix dish detergent with tempera paints. Paint outdoor things on window glass!
- Write to grandparents. Tell them about your indoor activity week!

Turkey Week

- Read a turkey report!
- Collect the word "turkey" from newspapers and magazines. Glue them into the shape of a turkey.
- How many can you think of...? A turkey gobbles. A cat meows. A whale ___ A giraffe ___ (Keep going!)
- Draw a picture of a turkey. Cut it apart to make a puzzle!
- How many other animals have turkey attributes? fanned tail claws?? long neck fat (indoor/outdoor)
- Write a turkey riddle!
- If a turkey could talk, what would it say two days after Thanksgiving?

Native American Week

- Use a U.S. map to locate the major Indian tribes of the 1600-1700s.
- Draw depicting scenes of early U.S. Indian...
- Plan an Indian food to include in your dinner tonight.
- Research an Indian craft of your area. Try it!
- Learn an Indian game to teach your friends.
- Enjoy an Indian poem or story today.
- Read a story about a famous American Indian!

December

A week to fold ---
What are all the reasons you fold your hands?

- Enjoy a paper folding activity.
- Build a house. Experiment with different textures to make them. Some houses...
- Prepare a recipe in which you have to fold ingredients.
- Make a collage of different lots of materials that have been folded.
- Design a folder to use for a specific purpose!
- Help fold the laundry.

Evergreen Week
How many evergreens can you list?

- Define "evergreen". Chart how many are in your yard or neighborhood.
- Learn all you can about it! Adopt a tree.
- Make a mirror... showing an animal... Is it like an evergreen?
- Make texture rubbings of different parts of an evergreen.
- Can trees native to warm climates be evergreen?
- Find out how to say "evergreen" in other languages.

Candle Week
Categorize all the candles you have in your house!

- Investigate all the ways to make candles... Choose one and try it!
- Compare burning time of smooth and twisted candles.
- What are all the other uses for wax?
- Visit a candle shop... enjoy the scents!
- Try putting luminaries along your walk tonight!
- With a grown-up, drip candle wax onto paper to make animal silhouettes.

Cookie Week
Plan a cookie-exchange party!

- List your favorite ingredients for cookies!
- Experiment! Substitute ingredients in a cookie recipe.
- Collect your favorite recipes for filled, bar, cut, drop cookies.
- Make cost comparisons along the cookie aisles of several grocery stores.
- Make ten gingerbread cookies - Decorate each one differently.
- Enjoy a fireside picnic ...with cookies for dessert!

Ribbons Week
Make a mobile with different ribbons.

- Compare kinds of ribbons... typewriter, hair, etc.
- How many different kinds of bows can you create with ribbons?
- Keep track of how much ribbon you use during the holiday season.
- Recycle your ribbon for re-use... or for ribbon creatures!
- What things can you use the word "ribbon" to describe? highway? river?...
- Have a ribbon-cutting ceremony!

January

J is January Week
- Search the newspaper for lots of different styles of J!
- What are all the things you can draw beginning with a J-shape? umbrella? bird? nose on a face?
- What things might be improved by being in the shape of a J? Why?
- Make alliterative sentences with J! Judy jumped just as...
- What are multiple meanings of /j/? jaywalk? bluejay?
- What are all the names it rhymes with?

Crayon Week
- Organize all your loose crayons.
- Shave old crayons — iron the shavings between wax paper. (Ask a grown-up to help!)
- Cut the wax paper into January shapes for mobiles or suncatchers!
- Make a pictionary. List all the colors! Name something for each color!
- Research how crayons are made!
- Explore making different lines and textures. Use your favorite ones to design a note or greeting card!
- Make your own book about colors.

Humanitarianism Week
- Look up the word humanitarian. List related words.
- Do something that is helpful to your neighbor!
- Check your library for information about famous humanitarians.
- Create a shadow box museum of artifacts that describes one of the humanitarians.
- Identify a local humanitarian effort!
- Outline a picture of a famous humanitarian with his/her characteristics.
- Monitor the newspaper for needy areas. Locate them on a map.

Tracks Week
- Look for animal tracks. Make a plaster cast of one!
- Find a book that shows animal tracks.
- Make an abstract picture using animal tracks in the design!
- Take a walk — leave tracks.
- See if a friend can follow your tracks!
- What kind of tracks do you leave? Knowingly? crumbs? your coat? extra dishes?
- Find out how detectives "track" people.
- Make a word puzzle using the different meanings of the word "track".

Halves Week
- The school year is half over! List accomplishments so far!
- Make a shapes collage in which every shape is cut in half!
- Plan a meal in which everything is cut in half.
- List things you can buy in halves — half pound, yard, dozen, etc!
- Fill a variety of containers half full — compose a musical selection!
- Think of how many things you've done halfway. Compare stories with a friend.
- Read a good book — read the second half!

February

Shadow Week Write a Groundhog's Day story. My shadow...	Go outside to measure your shadow at different times of the day!	Make up a dance to go with the song "Me and My Shadow".	Find out what a shadow box is ...and make one!	Make a matching game of objects and shadows.	Experiment with different materials to make unusual shadows!	Hang up a sheet... Create a shadow play!
Heart Week Design a piece of valentine clothing!	Make a heart-shaped potato print to decorate cards or wrapping paper.	Go on a search to find heart shapes!	Make a heart-shaped jigsaw puzzle.	Write a secret message using a heart code!	Deliver a valentine to someone who wouldn't be expecting one from you!	Categorize all the valentines you received!
Presidents Week Find out the requirements for being President. What's your opinion?	Cut out George Washington from newspaper ads to make a big collage!	What do other countries call their leaders? How many different titles can you find?	You President White House Washington, D.C. Write a letter to the current President of the USA.	Visit your library to find a book about a past president.	List 10 important things you'd accomplish if you were president.	How many facts can you list about your school?
Facts Week How many facts can you state about yourself? Write them on a profile of yourself.	Play a game that involves facts! Clue? Battleship? Facts in 5	Read a non-fiction book!	Critique TV commercials for facts and opinions.	See what facts are on your favorite cereal box.	Share an unusual fact with a friend.	
Indoor Sports Week Enjoy a sack race with heavy-weight trash bags.	Play a shoebox game with stuffed socks.	Invent an indoor sport using kitchen tools.	With an adult's help, carve Ivory Soap into different shapes... Have a floating soap race in your bathtub.	Map out an obstacle course in your house or garage.	Play balloon volleyball!	Create a boardgame based upon an outdoor sport.

March

Windy Week	Visit a weather station. Write a report about show what you found out about wind!	Make a list of good things and bad things to do on a windy day.	Investigate toys that use wind. Design a toy of your own.	Collect poems about the wind.	Pretend you're in a hot air balloon... What adventures could you have?	Survey people who have wind chimes. Make a graph to show the different kinds.
Design a hat that won't come off in the wind!						
March Week	Create a rhythm band to accompany your favorite!	List all the places you might see marching. parade? football game?	Read about John Philip Sousa. Why is he the "march king"?		Write a rhyme that you could say while marching.	Write some sentence with the word march. Substitute other words - amble, strut...
Check your library for recordings of marches. Enjoy! Then...						
St. Patrick's Week	Who was St. Patrick?	Make a button to wear!	Play a hide-the-shamrock game with your friends.	Make some leprechaun stick puppets.	Create a meal using shamrock-shaped food. pizza? pancakes?	Make a diorama of a leprechaun's hiding place.
What do you think a leprechaun looks like? Draw a picture.						
Change Week	What other changes, besides weather, affect us? Survey friends to find who does does not like change.	What are the other meanings of the word change?	Count the change in your parents' pockets. (Ask first!)	What changes do you look forward to in the next week, month, year?	Who have you change regularly?	What is something that you would like to change? What can you do about it?
March is a month of weather change. Describe why.						
Open Windows Week	Make a "window" terrarium...	Keep track of the temperature by the window and inside the room. Graph your observations.	Take a neighborhood walk — Notice everyone's windows!	Make a suncatcher with cardboard, tissue paper, and waxed paper.	Draw a scene from your open window.	Help your parents wash windows!
What changes do you notice when the window is open?						

April

National Library Week						
Visit your local library. Discover _facts_ about it.	Organize _your_ books into a personal library.	Trade a good book with a friend!	List books that have been made into movies.	Do something nice for your school librarian.	Check out something from the library that you've never tried before!	Research the history of public libraries in the U.S.A.
April means "to open". Why is opening associated with April?	Make a picture of things that is "opening" in April! reveal parts of April	Open a magazine at random... and start reading!	What are all the tools people use to open things?	Have a Grand Opening for ___!	Investigate _natural_ openings — caves, springs, etc.	Collect pictures of different architectural openings.
Egg Week Read "The Goose That Laid the Golden Egg". What would _you_ do if you found one?!	What are all the animals that lay eggs?	Make up a code using an egg shape.	Make up a game using egg cartons.	Make a word search puzzle of compound words that have "egg" in them.	Draw something in a egg shape... & cut it & puzzle!	Fix a fancy egg dish for a family meal.
Baskets Week What are all the things you put in baskets?	Research basketweaving. What materials do you have at home that would be good for basketweaving?	Make a Basket!	Think of some _famous_ baskets! Little Red Riding Hood, a tisket a tasket, Moses	Compare/ Contrast baskets in your home... Size, shape, color, use...	Hang a basket of bird seed in a tree.	Visit a natural history museum. Note which cultures used baskets.
April Showers Week April showers bring ___. How many ideas?	What effects do showers have? indoor activities, muddy boots, etc!	What else (besides water) would you like it to shower? flowers, good luck, etc!	What are different words that go with shower? List them on a raindrop mobile.	Name 10 activities for which you would _not_ want it to be raining. (sunbathing, etc.)	Hope for clear skies tonight — Look for different kinds of things in the sky!	Design a science experiment using drops of water.

Painting Week — Assemble different types of paint.	Paint the same picture with different types of paint. How does the picture change?	Paint pictures using different objects as stencils & brushes.	Paint on different kinds of paper — newspaper, bags, paper towels, etc.	Help with a painting project around the house!	Write a story to go with your favorite painting!	Check out the occupations associated with different kinds of painting.
Music Week — Survey family and friends for their favorite types of music.	Play a different type of music each evening at dinnertime.	Interview a musician.	Check out musical recordings from your library!	Identify all the different types of musical groups... quartets, chorus, etc.	Have a family sing-along of favorite songs.	Look for a concert to attend!
Mother's Day — Treat your mom to a wish of her choice!	Write a poem about your Mom is an Outstanding Teacher, Hugger,... E R	Brag about your mother- Make a poster!	Make a recording of all the different ways you show your mom.	Leave a note for your mom where she will find it!	A list of your mother's jobs... Offer to help!	Make a special card for your grandmother!
Pet Week — Spend extra time with your pet today!	Collect pictures of your pet. Make a book!	Make a puppet that looks like your pet.	Fix a special treat for your pet.	Make up a song about your pet!	Make a timeline of your pet's life. born 1/82 joined family 3/82	Have a pet party or Pet Show with your friends.
Memories Week — What's your best memory of each season of the past year?	With your family, plan a way to celebrate Memorial Day that will be memorable!	Spend ten minutes writing down all the funny memories you can think of. Share with your family!	Look through photo albums!	Make a memory quilt with fabric crayons.	What are your memories of favorite books, movies, TV shows?	Make a meal of old favorites!

June – July – August

Sundays: Games/Sports	Mondays: Reading	Tuesdays: Math	Wednesdays: Art	Thursdays: Science	Fridays: Fieldtrips	Saturdays: Social Studies
Enjoy a team sport today.	Start a chart that shows the types of reading you do this summer!	Measure! lengths, volumes, weights,...	Fingerpaint with pudding or shaving cream!	Start a science journal of observations.	Visit your local park to play!	Study a map of your community... Locate businesses, residential areas, etc.
Plan a fitness hike today.	Have an hour-long reading marathon— Read as many different kinds of things as you can!	Practice your math facts! + − = ×	Make a sunprint!	Read about a famous scientist!	Tour a factory or working business.	Make a timeline of your family's history.
Learn some games that you can play by yourself!	Choose an occupation— Chart how reading is important!	Research times of important events in your life!	Create a collage with things in nature!	Explore using a scientific object— magnifying glass, magnets, prism, etc!	Ride your bike somewhere!	How are your favorite cartoons alike and different from real life?
Invent a game using shadows.	Check your library for summer incentive reading programs!	Go on a pretend shopping spree through a catalogue with a calculator!	Make a puppet with scrap materials.	Find a science experiment you'd like to try!	Re-visit a school field-trip site with your family.	Plan patriotic family activities.
Learn a game from another country!	Read all the books written by a favorite author!	Survey summer leisure preferences— Graph results!	Enjoy a papier-mâché project!	Find a book about scientific myths!	Explore a historic site or museum!	Describe a typical morning from different points of view— Mom's, a pet's, a fly on the wall, etc.

1

Back to School

ESTABLISHING THE PHYSICAL ENVIRONMENT

When considering the total time spent in our classrooms, they could be thought of as second homes. Therefore the basic environment that is established at the beginning of the year warrants special consideration.

Why not take a new look at your classroom environment this year and envision it from the perspective of a child. After initially arranging the furniture and learning areas, get down on your knees and take a second look! Ask yourself these questions:

- How inviting is the room? How much will it appeal to children?
- Are the areas clearly defined?
- Are the "decorations" truly meaningful? Is the total effect too busy?
- Do the materials give clues to their use?
- Is the use of color varied?
- Does the furniture lend itself to the activity planned?
- What is permanent? What will be changed periodically?
- Can a choice of activity be made?
- Will the management of materials and activities suit the group's maturity and academic ability?

Call in an expert! Ask the opinion of your former students or another child you know. Make your room a special one for each child to experience on his or her first day back from summer vacation!

PERSONIFY THE ROUTINE

Choose a character or theme for the year and base bulletin board displays, birthday celebrations, class activities, and special events on that character or theme throughout the year. Consider asking the children to choose a mascot for the year. They will enjoy taking part in classroom challenges and celebrating special events when sponsored by . . .

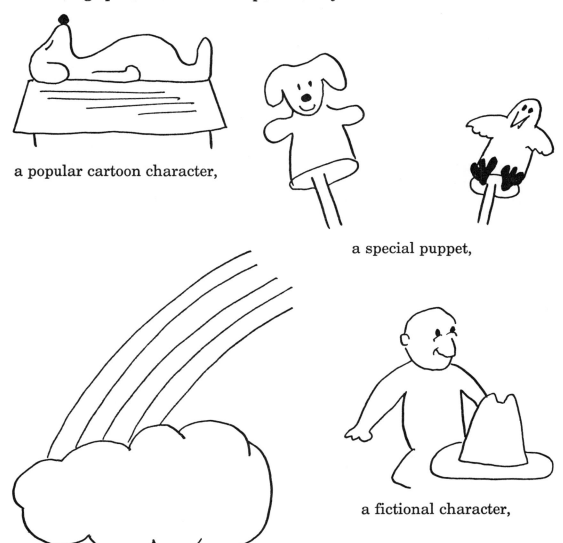

a popular cartoon character,

a special puppet,

a fictional character,

or, something whimsical like rainbows, dragons, unicorns, etc.

TEACHING ACTIVITIES

GETTING TO KNOW YOU . . .

Fluency

Have students make a long list of all the things they are interested in and all the things they like to do. Provide time for sharing the results. Chart common interests and consider forming interest clubs.

Flexibility

Spend time having the students get to know the faculty too—buddy children up to interview all the staff members. Summarize information on a bulletin board for the whole class to enjoy.

Elaboration

Do your students know the meanings of their names? Do they know why they were named what they are? Can they tie the meaning of their name into a personal fact about themselves? Explore different name resources. Have children compile a family tree of names or have them make a list of favorite names.

Originality

Rather than prepare beginning of the year nametags, ask children to design their own. You'll quickly discover some interesting facts about your new class and the children will enjoy a creative activity as a start-up for the new year.

Observation

On the first few days of school, create a getting-to-know-you class book. Have children record physical features (hair color, dimples, looks just like Mom and Dad, etc.) on a silhouette page. Follow each silhouette with the child's response to affective questions such as:

- What are three things about yourself that you are proud of?
- Tell about the most interesting place you've ever visited.
- Who's your favorite performer?
- If you had a chance to have three wishes granted, what would they be? Why?

Assemble the book and allow class members to check it out overnight for home sharing.

Create a door-sized word search puzzle composed of all the names of your new students. How quickly do students find and learn each other's names?

ALPHABET FUN

Fluency

Choose a consonant from the alphabet. Brainstorm all the school items that begin with that sound. List or draw them.

Flexibility

Of what does the shape of the letters remind you? Hide as many letters as you can in a picture. Share your picture with a friend and enjoy identifying the letters.

Originality

Design original alphabet letters. Stretch your thinking! Mr. M might be a mouse or a mushroom maniac!

Elaboration

Choose a favorite character designed for a letter of the alphabet and alliterate a sentence or story for that character. For example:

Mr. M the mouse munches more mangoes in May.

Research different alphabets and make a timeline of the one that intrigues you most.

Observation

Look at the physical surroundings. What letters can you see hidden in chairs, desks, cinder block walls, etc. Write clues for other students to solve and discover the letters you located. For example:

You'll find me in the branch of a tree . . .
I'm the letter ———— .

Consider: Which letter configurations are similar? Why? Which are different? Why? What other alphabets have been invented? How are they similar to ours? How are they different?

Write your name with different alphabet styles. Explain why each would be appropriate for a specific purpose. Which would you use on a job application, return address, or on an art project?

LOOKING AT NUMBERS . . .

Fluency

How many ways can you make the number five?

Flexibility

How many different ways are numbers used in your environment? Look at the clock, wall, equipment, people's clothes, and so on. List them or make a poster.

Elaboration

Have someone really interested in numbers? Invite them to research number systems, number patterns, number relationships to music, art, or astronomy!

Originality

Design some number codes for your students to solve. Ask them to reciprocate and design a code for you!

Observation

List things in your classroom by a number count. Record them in a number book.

> I see one _____ ,
> two _____ ,
> etc.

SCHOOL BUILDINGS

Fluency

Have children make a list of all the good things about your school building. Suggest that they include their list in a letter to their grandparents telling about the start of the new year.

Flexibility

Invite students to draw a picture of a favorite spot in the school building. Then draw that same spot as it might look to a parent, a pencil lying on the floor, or a person who has never been to your school.

Originality

Design a pennant for your school.

Elaboration

Make a mobile of school personnel. Be sure to include the tools they use and other interesting details.

Observation
Draw a floor plan of your school. Show the paths that you walk each day.

CLASSMATES

Fluency
What are all the nice things classmates can do for each other? Make a collage of your ideas.

Flexibility
Make a list of your attributes as a "classmate" (for example: willing to lend a pencil, great for a buddy project, etc.). Make a chart or poster of your ideas. Which ones do you think your classmates would like the best?

Originality
Consider the ways in which classmates resemble a large family. What things are the same? Write an original story or play about this idea to share.

Elaboration
Use every classmates' initials to create an elaborate design!

Observation
"How many classmates ride a bus?"

"How many classmates are taller than you?"

What kinds of "How many . . ." questions can you compose about classmates?

Write a list, collect the answers, and put them together in a book.

LABOR DAY

Fluency
Make a very long list of all the occupations you encounter throughout your day.

Flexibility
Turn the tables! What if children had careers and adults went to school? Write about your ideas.

Originality

Create a diorama that reflects a certain occupation. Be sure to include lots of details specific to that occupation.

Elaboration

Sponsor an occupations party at which everyone dresses as a different occupation. Plan the refreshments and activities along the theme of occupations. For example, use refrigerator cookie dough and have children design cookie shapes to go with specific occupations—police officer's badge, secretary's computer, builder's hammer.

Observation

During the workday, interview adults about jobs. Write a detailed description of their responsibilities. Compile each classmate's findings into a career catalog. Take a poll of career interests. Which career is most popular? Least popular?

HOW TO USE THE WORKSHEETS

TEACHING SUGGESTIONS

Here are suggestions for using each of the reproducible student worksheets that appear on pages 31–35. These are preceded by a management sheet you can use to keep track of children's activities.

Back to School! Contract/Home Project Activities (Fluency)

This worksheet lists seven independent activities that may be directly assigned, given as extra credit, or sent home for enrichment.

Famous Facts About Me Inventory (Observation)

Consider using this worksheet as a means of getting to know student interests at the beginning of the year. Tie it in during the year by writing autobiographies from the information, basing independent studies on student interests, or adapting it as an interview sheet for finding out about someone else.

Initially Speaking (Fluency)

Before assigning this worksheet, model brainstorming words from initials. As a class, string the words together in sentences. After using the idea with the whole class, students should be ready to try it independently.

This Year I'd Like to . . . (Originality)

Often students have special things they'd like to accomplish during the year. Use this worksheet to allow them to express their special wishes. As the year progresses, help each child realize at least one wish.

"That's Me!" Name Tally (Observation)

Introduce skills of bar graphing by keying into children's names. During a specific day, children keep track of how often they hear their names and the reasons why they are called. As a class, summarize reasons for calling people by name and then ask the children to transfer the collected data to the bar graph.

Back-to-School Management Sheet

Names	Back to School!	Famous Facts About Me	Initially Speaking . . .	This Year I'd Like to . . .	That's Me!

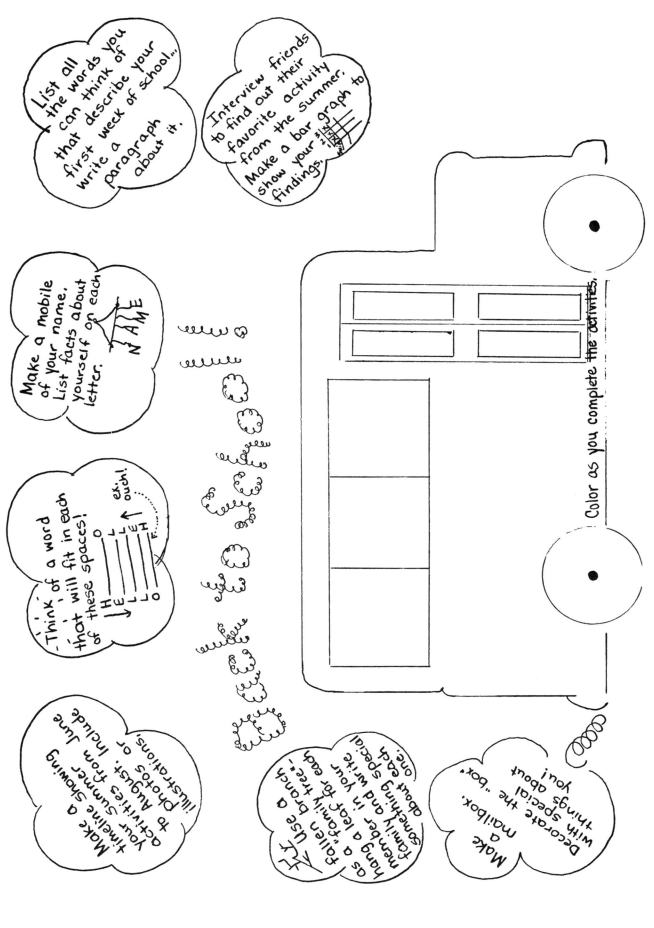

Famous Facts About Me
Inventory

People in my family:

Pets:

Places I've lived:

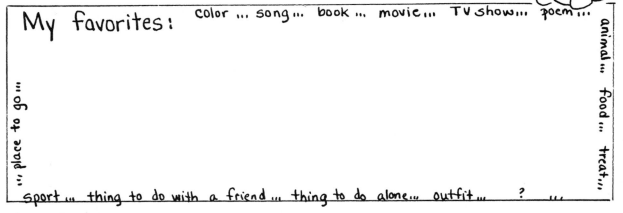

My favorites: color ... song ... book ... movie ... TV show ... poem ...

... place to go ...

animal ... food ... treat ...

sport ... thing to do with a friend ... thing to do alone ... outfit ... ? ...

My hobbies:

Things I collect:

Something I'm really good at:

Something new I'd like to learn:

Now ... try organizing these ideas into a poster about yourself!

Name _____

Initially Speaking...

"...M.S."

What are your initials?

List words that start with your initials!

Saw said Sail

mat mug more

Use your words to write a story!

This year I'd like to...

☺ _____
_____
_____
_____

☺ _____
_____
_____

Think of things you've never done before that you'd like to do this year- list them!

☺ _____
_____
_____
_____

☺ _____
_____
_____

That's Me!

How often do you hear your name during the school day? Keep a tally in the boxes below ... then summarize your findings in the bar graph.

✓	reason name called	✓	reason name called	✓	reason name called

Number of times name called

12						
11						
10						
9						
8						
7						
6						
5						
4						
3						
2						
1						

Reasons

Bulletin Board Ideas

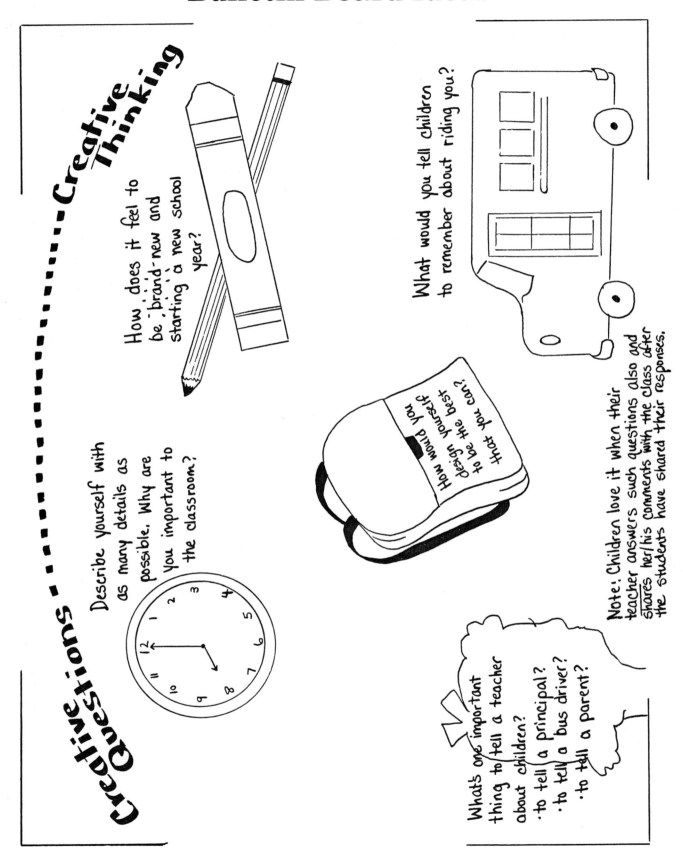

Creative Thinking

Creative Questions

How does it feel to be brand-new and starting a new school year?

What would you tell children to remember about riding you?

Describe yourself with as many details as possible. Why are you important to the classroom?

How would you design yourself to be the best that you can?

What's one important thing to tell a teacher about children?
• to tell a principal?
• to tell a bus driver?
• to tell a parent?

Note: Children love it when their teacher answers such questions also and shares her/his comments with the class after the students have shared their responses.

Categorically Thinking ...

school's or teacher's name	a school activity or subject	a school supply	a place in our school	a person in our school	an adjective that describes our school	Your own idea!
m	math		noisy cafeteria		new	
e		eraser		adult helper		

Fill in the categories with words or pictures!

After the class completes the bulletin board grid, provide time for students to make individual grids.

Soar Into September...

Ask children to draw a Summer object and write about their Summer on that shape.

What are all the flying things your class can name? Allow children to design their own nametag with the criteria that it must be something that flies.

After names have been learned, suspend the nametags in the room and hang children's work from them.

A secret about me is...

Something I hope to accomplish this year is...

Something I learned last year that will help this year is...

Post these divergent questions—children respond in graffiti style or with illustrations.

Up, Up and Away! Hooray for First Grade! Have children they are excited about. List things children decorate on kites—hang and for display.

PARENT CONNECTIONS

Set up a positive communication network with parents right from the beginning. Established avenues of communication facilitate a year-long exchange that benefits children both at home and at school.

- Send home a Parent Observation sheet of the student. Elicit parent responses to such things as their child's interests, strengths, weaknesses, unique experiences, etc. Utilize the information when planning classroom activities.

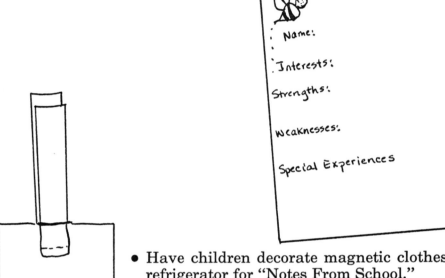

- Have children decorate magnetic clothespins to put on their home refrigerator for "Notes From School."

- Prepare dittoed checklists that list behaviors important to classroom management and student achievement and send them home daily or weekly. Encourage parents to return them with a comment of their own.

- Send home a teacher's "wish list" that explains specific tasks and needs that parents could help with through the year. Parents will be more willing to help when looking at a specific task list as they can then accurately assess whether or not they have the resources needed.

Try these September activities for immediately involving the parents in their child's learning activities:

- Conduct a summer activities survey by sending the following form home. Compile the results in a class bar graph and have children illustrate their favorite summer activity.

Dear Parents:

Please help with a bar graph activity by checking the appropriate boxes that apply to your summer. Give additional information where possible.

Thank you!

This summer, we . . .

☐ stayed "in state"
      special visits?

☐ went out of state to . . .

☐ cooked something together
      which was . . .

☐ read a book in an unusual place
      which was . . .

☐ crafted something together
      item:

☐ did something we've never done before!

☐ saw a movie as a family
      title:

☐ enjoyed the following indoor activities:

☐ enjoyed the following outdoor activities:

- Ask students to create a collage at home to share with the class. The collage should be all about themselves: their favorite color, song, book, magazine, comic book character, room to enjoy, piece of furniture, sport, thing to do when bored, animal, and so on. Share the collages by posting them on bulletin boards and by providing discussion time during which everyone tries to guess the identity of each artist.
- Recruit parent volunteers NOW! Survey interests—strictly clerical help (dittoes, filing, typing) or interest in working with individual children, with groups of students, on special projects (crafts, talent areas), on foreign languages, and so on. Sustain volunteers' interest throughout the year by providing variety within preferred task areas.

VOLUNTEERS...

	Mrs. Possum	Mrs. Otter
Week 1	type vocabulary word lists	drill vocabulary words with students
Week 2	cut borders and bulletin board letters	record dictated stories
Week 3		

2

Fall

TEACHING ACTIVITIES

FALL POETRY

Fluency

Ask each child to have a poem ready to share for a poetry break sometime during the day.

Flexibility

Leave out the rhyming words as you read poems to the class. Let students supply the word as the poem is read.

Originality

Have students create masks to accompany favorite poems. Write poems on the back of the masks. Students hold the masks in front of their faces while they read their poems.

Elaboration

Students write a poem about a particular object, draw that object, and then copy the poem as an outline of their drawing.

Observation

Write a rebus poem.

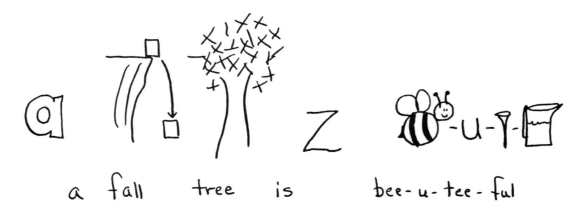

a fall tree is bee-u-tee-ful

JOHNNY APPLESEED

Fluency

List all the things you can make with an apple—applesauce, apple snacks, apple print, pomander ball, candle holder, etc. Send the list home as home project ideas.

Flexibility

Discuss the changes one sees in an apple tree through the seasons. Take the point of view of the tree. How does each season make you feel?

Originality

Survey the class for favorite apple recipes. Have children write how to prepare their favorite apple dish in their own sequence. Compile their writings into a class apple cookbook.

Elaboration

Research different types of apples and compile information about each in a group chart. Use the names of the different apples in tall tales about apple growing, picking, cooking, and so on. Example:

"Granny Smith and Her McIntosh"
"Jonathan, the Smartest Apple Ever"

Observation

Note attributes of apples. Ask everyone to bring an apple to school. Group the apples in different ways. Discuss the various sizes, shapes, and colors. List the attributes in a chart, and compare the apples to other things that are the same/different.

ADVENTURES

Fluency

Make a long list of adventurous careers. Research one!

Flexibility

Be adventuresome! Explore a new section of the library.

Originality

Dramatize an adventure story that you and your friends create.

Elaboration

Read a book about Christopher Columbus. Illustrate a timeline of his life.

Observation

Take an imaginative adventure walk through your neighborhood.

SAFETY

Fluency

Collect materials from the library, utility companies, and other sources. Have students look through the materials and think about safety in all kinds of weather—lightning, flooding, blizzards, etc. Then invite students to make accordion-fold booklets showing "Safety in All Types of Weather."

Flexibility

Have students choose a favorite fairy tale or nursery rhyme. Illustrate something "unsafe" in the selection, and show how it could be changed to be "safe."

Originality

Provide a variety of materials for students to use in creating a three-dimensional safety project. Show an important idea about safety through projects such as mobiles, cubes, puppets, dioramas, sculptures, and so on.

Elaboration

Have students draw a picture of a playground that includes five unsafe things. Be tricky! Add enough details to the picture so friends will really have to hunt to find what's wrong!

Observation

Take a quiet walk through the school to compile a "safety count" of items such as fire extinguishers, fire alarms, railings, exit signs, wet floor signs, crosswalks, etc. What conclusions can you draw about safety in your school?

FALL WORDS

Fluency

Brainstorm lists of words appropriate to different fall topics, including safety, Columbus Day, harvest, Halloween, magic, and United Nations Day. Display word lists on related shapes. Encourage children to continue thinking of words that might be added.

Flexibility

Which words fit more than one shape? Which words would be appropriate for other seasons of the year?

Originality

Create a word puzzle, riddle, writing, or poem using words from a word list.

Elaboration

Think of a unique way to share your writing. Examples: model of Columbus's ship or a magic show.

Observation

Conduct a word study. Which words from the fluency list plug into language skills you have studied.

HOW TO USE THE WORKSHEETS

TEACHING SUGGESTIONS

Here are suggestions for using each of the reproducible student worksheets that appear on pages 48–51. These are preceded by a management sheet you can use to keep track of children's activities.

Home Project (Fluency, Observation)

Use this worksheet centering on autumn changes for home enrichment.

September Word Search (Fluency)

Introduce to the class how to combine words into a word search puzzle. Children can then use this worksheet to create their own September word lists and word search puzzles. Older students may want to fill in the extra spaces with random symbols or letters. Younger students may wish to leave the extra spaces blank.

Fall Activities List (Fluency)

This is a good worksheet to assign to "buddies" because children's fluency increases when paired with a friend. *Hint:* Team reluctant writers with students who enjoy writing!

Fall Management Sheet

Names	Home Project	September Word Search	Fall Activities List		

List all the changes that occur during the fall season:

HOME PROJECT

Collect lists from your friends.

Organize their ideas into a graph ...

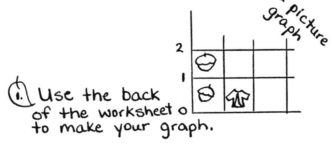

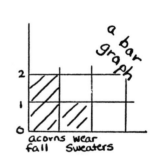

a picture graph

a bar graph

acorns fall wear sweaters

1. Use the back of the worksheet to make your graph.

2. List the fall changes **across** the bottom of your graph.

3. List the number of people who noted each change **down** the left side of your graph.

Look for the most common ideas... and the most unusual!

Name _____

September Word Search

1. List words that make you think of September.
2. Arrange the words in the grid below... ask a friend to solve your word search!

_____   _____   _____

_____   _____   _____

_____   _____   _____

Name _____

Can i can, calling!
all fluent thinkers!

FIRST... make a very long list of all the great things
to do in the fall:

Can you think of
other ways to classify
your ideas?
List them on the
back of your paper.

NEXT... put an "x" on the things you can do
only in the fall.
Put a ★ on things you enjoy every fall.

Bulletin Board Ideas

Write a detailed description of your teacher and the classroom...tuck it away to read again at the end of the year.

Make up a poem or riddle about your new school supplies.

Construct a counting bulletin board or flannel board activity depicting school items... volunteer to present it to a first grade or kindergarten class.

Write a shape book about your first week of school. Include a page for each day.

Call a new friend from your class.

Invent a safety and school manners game. Write situation cards that require players to make choices. Build in consequences for incorrect choices.

Create stand-up figures of school helpers.

Survey and report - What did friends look forward to in coming back to school?

Duplicate the above bus pattern for each student, as they complete activities they color in the corresponding space on the bus. Post a large bus on a bulletin board... as children complete activities they sign the space on the large classroom bus.

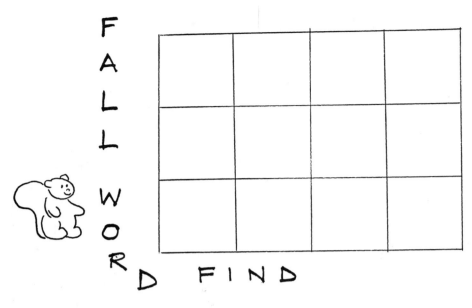

F
A
L
L
W
O
R
D
FIND

Bulletin Board Word Find

Create a bulletin board sized word find! Post a large grid and have students fill in fall words. Trade it with another class . . . and challenge them to solve it.

Use the pictures below by enlarging them to bulletin board size. Reproduce the acorns, have students color them, list the words from the word find puzzle on them, and use them as a border for the bulletin board.

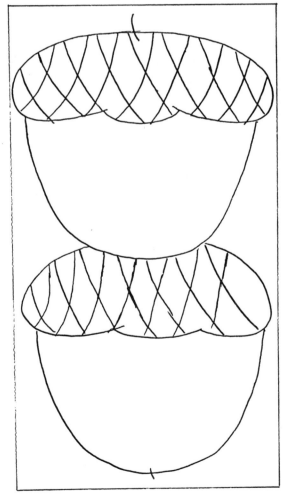

1-January
2-February
3-March
4-April
5-May
6-June
7-July
8-August
9-September
10-October
11-November
12-December

Birds migrate.

People wear sweaters.

10

Windows stay closed.

Fall... 8, 9, 10!

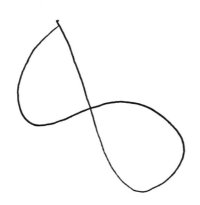

8 — 9 — 10 Doodle Board

Challenge children to illustrate fall happenings, ideas, and changes while hiding an "8," "9," or "10" in their pictures.

As an extra challenge, give children a piece of paper with 8, 9, or 10 printed randomly on it and encourage them to create their fall picture by incorporating the number.

PARENT CONNECTIONS

FALL

Suggest that students pursue a "Leaf Study" around their homes. How many different colors of leaves can they find? What are their shapes? Sizes? Colors? Survey! What are the many things that families do with their leaves?

Help students make a plan to record and graph weather information (temperature, precipitation, etc.) for a month.

3

Halloween

TEACHING ACTIVITIES

TENS (October is the tenth month)

Fluency

How many "tens" can you count? Think of sequential sets and identify the tenth member of each. Examples include: volumes of encyclopedias, things on a shelf, houses on a street, and chapters in a book.

Flexibility

Find words that have "ten" in them (*ten*der, of*ten*). Write rebus clues for the words or compile them in a dictionary shaped like a ten.

Originality

Use the prefix "deci-" or "deca-" to make new words. For example:

decigrade = the average of your ten best grades
decabat = a ten-winged bat

Elaboration

Plan a party to celebrate the number ten. Serve ten favorite snacks, play a metric measurement game, sing a base ten song, have teams race while counting by tens, recognize the "Top Ten" of ——, etc.

Observation

Design an obstacle course based on the metric system. Include stations where students have to measure liquids and solids.

CAST A CREATIVE SPELL

Fluency

Brainstorm all the scary things you might hear during October. Cut the words out of large pieces of paper. Divide the class into committees to illustrate on the cut-out words things that might make that scary sound or statement.

Flexibility

Discuss the meaning of the phrase "on the other hand" with the class. Then consider Halloween things in the time frame of summer. Example: Sheets make great ghost costumes. On the other hand, a sheet is all you want on your bed in summer because it is so hot.
Try pumpkin, ghost, treat, monster, candle, etc.!

Originality

Create a classroom Halloween store with products that children have redesigned. Ask them to bring in cereal boxes, soap containers, candy wrappers, and so on. Cover the product name with construction paper and then create a Halloween-related product name and illustration such as Scary O's or Choke-a-Cola.
After the center is set up, have students invent a set of "monster money" to role play buying and selling.

Elaboration

Ask children to bring in a board game or card game that they already know how to play. Then challenge students to change the characterization or setting of the game to a Halloween theme. Pair children to teach each other their spooky games!

Observation

Have children make a leaf print or texture rubbing. Set projects aside for a day. The next day children take a second look at them by turning them in all sorts of different directions. Then they try to visualize a Halloween picture and add details with black tempera paint or markers.

DIVERGENT DISGUISES

Fluency

Discuss and list all the times when one might need a disguise. Develop one situation into a very dramatic story.

Flexibility

Consider the costume's point of view. What is Halloween like? Write diary entries for a costume for October 30 through November 1.

Originality

Collect enough grocery bags for each student and set up a disguise center! Include a variety of materials (pipe cleaners, feathers, yarn, pompoms, fiberfill, glitter, coat hangers, tinsel, aluminum foil, etc.) that the children can use to create an original disguise.

Elaboration

How can musical sound be used to enhance a disguise? Provide a variety of musical instruments to experiment with sounds while the class brainstorms how the sounds could enhance a disguise.

Observation

Ask the librarian for help in locating books in which characters use disguises (*Miss Nelson Is Missing, Nate the Great*, etc.). As the books are read, discuss the illustrations. What do children notice about the disguises? Ask them to draw the disguised character changing only one detail. Who can quickly notice the change?

FOLD AWAY A HALLOWEEN CHARACTER

Fluency

Experiment with double fold, pinwheel fold, prism fold, and quilling to create a Halloween character.

Flexibility

Use your Halloween character to teach a language or math skill to another student.

Originality

Come up with a unique way to fold paper to create a character. Name the new kind of fold after yourself!

Elaboration

Plan a lesson to teach a younger group of children how to fold paper to create a Halloween character. What variety of materials (feathers, pompoms, aluminum foil, etc.) will add scary details?

Observation

Make a twin to your Halloween character. Change only a few details. See who can detect the differences!

HALLOWEEN STORY EXTENSIONS

Write a Halloween story, then extend the story with these ideas:

Fluency

Create a collage representing an aspect of the story that you can explore through all five senses. Consider as many sources of materials as possible (cereal boxes, magazines, newspapers, photographs, dried beans, popcorn, straws, string, buttons, etc.).

Flexibility

Create a three-dimensional project—sculpture, mobile, cube, diorama, etc.—to show the characters of the story.

Originality

Design a gameboard with cards that have comprehension questions about the story on them.

Elaboration

Make an elaborate mural to show important elements of the story.

Observation

Design an informational pamphlet or a picture puzzle to show the setting of the story.

HOW TO USE THE WORKSHEETS

TEACHING SUGGESTIONS

The following are suggestions for using each of the reproducible student worksheets on pages 61–67. These are preceded by a management sheet to help you record each child's activities.

Same/Different (Originality)

Children enjoy and benefit from visual discrimination exercises. Use this worksheet to have students create their own Halloween scenes in which they hide unusual details. Laminate the scenes, provide an erasable grease pencil, and organize as a center of activity.

Home Project (Flexibility)

For children who enjoy words and their multiple meanings, send home this enrichment idea. Encourage the whole family to participate and enjoy.

October Song (Originality)

Enjoy singing Halloween words to the tune of "Row, Row, Row Your Boat." Brainstorm October/Halloween words. Encourage children to substitute the words into familiar tunes to create original Halloween lyrics.

Haunting Comparisons (Flexibility)

Comparisons can be particularly challenging when looking for similarities between unlike things. Brainstorm with the class many unusual answers for the examples given. Children may wish to record one of the answers or try to think of an original response. This is also a good parent volunteer activity.

October Attributes (Flexibility)

For children who enjoy noting details and discovering unusual comparisons, try this worksheet. Consider pairing observant children with those who need to develop observation skills.

Halloween Disguises (Fluency)

Discuss disguises and have the children complete this worksheet listing as many ideas for the given materials as possible. For extension, encourage children to construct one disguise idea at home.

Halloween Comments (Originality)

Encourage children to consider Halloween from different points of view. They may wish to role play their responses using appropriate vocal expressions.

Halloween Management Sheet

Names	Same/ Different	Home Project	October Song	Haunting Comparisons	October Attributes	Halloween Disguises	Halloween Comments

Same- Different?

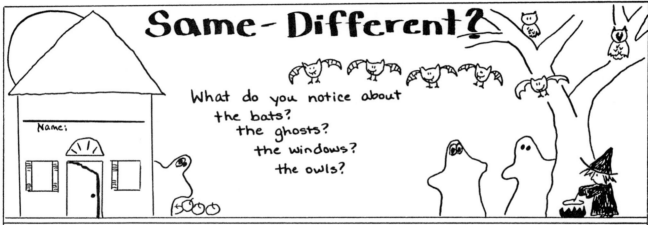

What do you notice about
the bats?
the ghosts?
the windows?
the owls?

Name:

Draw a Halloween picture below that has several bats, ghosts, witches and pumpkins in it. Make one member of each set different in some way. Ask a friend to find the differences!

Name _____

Can you fill this space
with October words?

Which words have
multiple meanings?

example: ghost- ghost of a chance
ghost writer
gho-straight home!

_____

_____

_____

_____

_____

_____

AN OCTOBER SONG

Boo, hiss, scare your friends
As you trick or treat
Run and scream and shout and cry
Tripping down the street!
(Sing to Row, Row, Row Your Boat)

Name _____

🦇 Substitute words into a familiar tune to create an October Song.

_____

Sing to the tune: _____

Haunting Comparisons

© 1990 by The Center for Applied Research in Education

Name _____

Compare Halloween characters to unusual things by thinking of ways they are alike.

A bat is like a __possum__ because __they both hang upside down__ .
A bat is like _____ because _____ .

A cat is like a __rubber band__ because __they both stretch__ .
A cat is like _____ because _____ .

An owl is like a __night watchman__ because _____ .
An owl is like _____ because _____ .

A scarecrow is like __a turkey__ because _____ .
A scarecrow is like _____ because _____ .

spider...skeleton...pumpkin...etc.

A _____ is like _____ because _____ .
A _____ is like _____ because _____ .

October Attributes

First Choose common objects-

pencil, paper clip, desk, _____

_____

List attributes -

pencil-	desk -	? _____ -	? _____ -
wooden	_____	_____	_____
long	_____	_____	_____
hexagonal	_____	_____	_____
colorful	_____	_____	_____
_____	_____	_____	_____

Who-o-o can list attributes?

Next, list October words:

harvest, tractor, autumn leaves, witch's hat,

Now, compare! Which common objects have the same attributes
as the October words?

pencil   and   witch's hat
because both are _pointy_

_____ and _____

because both are _____

_____ and _____

because both are _____

_____ and _____

because both are _____

_____ and _____

because both are _____

Name _____

Halloween Disguises—

What disguises could you make from...

a big cardboard box?

big and small tree branches?

fluffy and smooth yarn?

ooo _____
your idea! picture it here.

Name _____

© 1990 by The Center for Applied Research in Education

Name _____

Halloween Comments--

What comments would each of these have to make about Halloween?

Bulletin Board Ideas

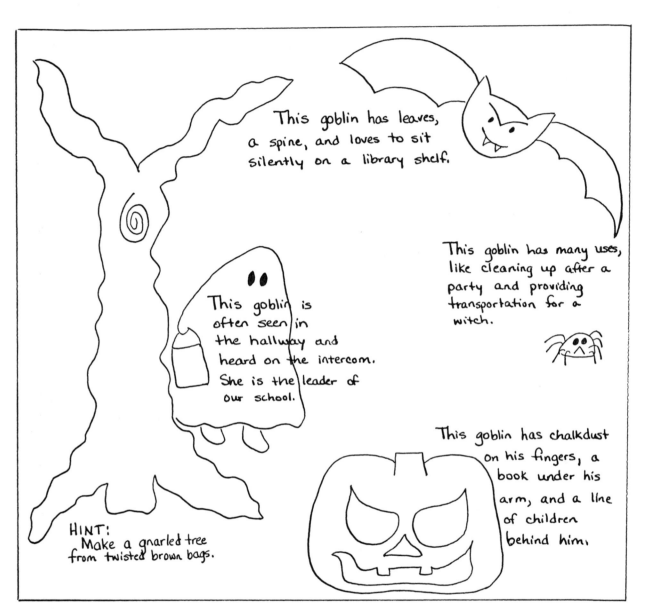

This goblin has leaves, a spine, and loves to sit silently on a library shelf.

This goblin has many uses, like cleaning up after a party and providing transportation for a witch.

This goblin is often seen in the hallway and heard on the intercom. She is the leader of our school.

This goblin has chalkdust on his fingers, a book under his arm, and a line of children behind him.

HINT: Make a gnarled tree from twisted brown bags.

⸮?Who's Haunting Our School⸮?

Sponsor a school-wide interactive bulletin board by posting riddles about October "things" on different student-made shapes. Create a flap somewhere on the shape and hide the answer to the riddle under the flap. Spark interest in the activity by announcing over the intercom that Hallway ___ has some mysteries in store for everyone! Encourage students to write riddles about any-*one* or any-*thing* that could be haunting the school (e.g., school helpers, school supplies, book characters, classmates, etc.). People will enjoy stopping by to read, ponder and discover the answers to the riddles by lifting the flaps on the different shapes.

PUMPKIN SURVEY

	plain	happy face	mean face	used other materials	
10					
9					
8					
7					
6					
5					
4					
3					
2					
1					

Directions: Use this sheet while taking a tour of your neighborhood with an adult. Categorize the pumpkins you see. How many are plain? How many are happy? Mean? How many have used other materials? Return this graph to school by _____ for class discussion. It will be posted on the bulletin board as a math extension.

Teacher: Use this sheet as a home project, then post children's surveys on a bulletin board as they are returned. Have them cut out pumpkins and pose math questions on the pumpkins. Encourage them to solve the questions as a math extension activity.

Example: How many plain pumpkins did everyone see in all? Which category had the most sightings?

TRICK OR TREAT—
Tasks on a Grid!

Make a bulletin board sized house with the items shown in a grid. Post the bat challenges and encourage children to complete them during their daily activity time.

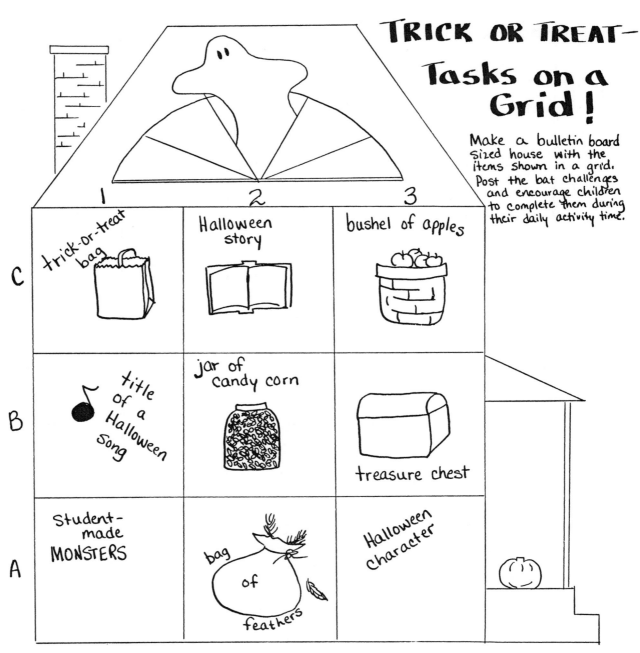

	1	2	3
C	trick-or-treat bag	Halloween story	bushel of apples
B	title of a Halloween song	jar of candy corn	treasure chest
A	Student-made MONSTERS	bag of feathers	Halloween character

🦇 Design a costume using A-2.

🦇 Write a story about A-1.

🦇 Make up a math problem using B-2 and C-3.

🦇 Paint an elaborate picture of A-3's home.

🦇 List safety rules to remember for C-1.

🦇 Sing B-1 with a friend.

🦇 Take time to enjoy C-2.

🦇 Plan where you might hide B-3 in the classroom. Draw a treasure map leading to it.

PARENT CONNECTIONS

HALLOWEEN

Ask students to create a maze in a shoebox as a home project. When the mazes are brought to school, connect them by cutting corresponding doors and stapling adjoining walls together. How big will the class maze grow? Can students find their way through using a monster pawn?

Projects suggested in the Teaching Activities and Calendar sections of this book lend themselves to promoting interaction among children and their parents. Provide choices of projects to be completed in a "Haunted Homework" contract. As the projects come in, be sure to allow time for sharing and reward students with special certificates of participation!

Ask children to create an original Halloween decoration at home— goblins, witches' home, footprints, weird recordings, disguised musical instruments, etc. Use these products to decorate your classroom!

Send home black and orange construction paper for Halloween home art projects. First, have children recreate their families' jack-o'-lantern face using the construction paper. Then have them use dried pumpkin seeds and construction paper to create a mosaic. Both projects should come back to school for an October display.

SAFETY

Ask children to talk about home safety with their parents and make a puppet who will report back to the class about the safety conversation. Encourage the use of props such as a safety checklist, an escape route map, a phone numbers list, etc., for use with the puppet report.

As you begin a unit of study on safety, send the following letter along with the home project sheet:

Dear Parents:

For the next _____ weeks, we will be doing lots of different activities that focus on safety. Watch for a Safety Cat homework sheet that your child will be using to check out various aspects of home safety. Please help him/her complete that sheet.

Additionally, I ask your help with a variety of family discussion topics. Each child will be bringing home an assigned topic to discuss with the family, summarize in a short paragraph, illustrate, and return to school. We are collecting these sheets to display on a class safety banner.

Thanks for your help as we extend our safety studies to the real world!

HOME SAFETY INVENTORY

Check your house for:

_____ flashlights with batteries

_____ smoke alarms with batteries

_____ fire extinguisher

_____ posted emergency phone numbers

_____ planned fire escape

_____ cleaning supplies properly stored

_____ no torn/frayed electrical wires

_____ no overloaded electrical outlets

_____ other: _____

_____   _____

Safety Cat Homework

4

Thanksgiving

TEACHING ACTIVITIES

FEAST ON MATH!

Fluency

Make a list of all the numbers associated with Thanksgiving. For example:

How many pieces of turkey will be eaten?

How many people will be visiting friends?

How many Pilgrims and Indians were at the first Thanksgiving?

Compile the numbers into a "Did you ever think . . ." book about Thanksgiving.

Flexibility

What kinds of patterns do you notice at Thanksgiving? Consider the food served each year, the place settings, the sequence of the day, etc. Predict what patterns will carry through this Thanksgiving.

Originality

Brainstorm the different "sets" that go with Thanksgiving—meats, vegetables, family, special serving dishes, etc. Ask children to illustrate the sets in a Thanksgiving mobile. As an extension, write math word problems using the sets.

Elaboration

Use skip counting as the basis for an elaborate list of things that could happen at Thanksgiving. Encourage exaggerated ideas! For example: On Thanksgiving Day, I ate *two* whole turkeys, sat at *four* different places at the table, called *six* friends to see how much they ate, etc. Tape record the children reading their descriptions with elaborate inflections!

Observation

Collect and display different grocery store ads that list Thanksgiving foods and prices. Discuss the different ways the ads are presented and the different types of pricing (by the pound, by the individual item, etc.). Complete a table that compares different pricing methods. What observations can be made?

NOTICING NOVEMBER

Fluency

Brainstorm with the class all the occasions for which a family might get together. List expected behaviors of family members and compile them into a "Manners for Family Gatherings" book.

Flexibility

Discuss the multiple meanings of different Thanksgiving words, such as feast, corn, or bowl. Challenge children to write a story that uses several meanings of the words.

Originality

Start a "party designs company" in your classroom by asking children to design coordinating banners, placemats, napkin rings, centerpieces, etc., for different family occasions. Divide into groups and create products for a class party.

Elaboration

Try this Thanksgiving Day drawing game! Students pair off and one partner selects a Thanksgiving object and draws it one detail at a time. The partner tries to guess what is being drawn with each added detail. How many guesses does it take to recognize the object? Trade roles and play again!

Observation

Ask children to choose three people to observe during their next family gathering. Children should notice things those people seemed to enjoy and things they liked least during the day. Then have children draw a detailed picture with descriptive labels of one of the people they observed.

"TH" IS FOR THANKSGIVING AND . . .

Fluency
Categorize the things in your room.
What's your *th*ird favorite Thanksgiving food?

Flexibility
Use a *th*imble for something other than a sewing project.

Originality
Write a *th*ank you note to your *Th*anksgiving dinner cook(s)!

Elaboration
Look up "*th*ankful" in a *th*esaurus. Make an elaborate poster to showcase the word.
Build a mini-*th*eater out of a shoebox.

Observation
Enjoy an art project with *th*ick and *th*in lines!

CRISP!

Fluency
List the ways November is crisp. Make a word search puzzle of words that go with "crisp."

Flexibility
What things are ruined when they become crisp?

Originality
Plan a luncheon for your friends and serve crisp things.
Create a puppet show in which a mystery is solved on a crisp November day.

Elaboration
Make a sound recording of crisp things breaking. See if your friends can identify the objects.

Observation
What changes do you have to make when the weather turns crisp?

ORANGE AND BROWN

Fluency
What things do you associate with November that are orange and brown? Classify them as natural things, food, clothing, and so on.

Flexibility
Cut out orange and brown pieces from magazine pictures. Use them to make a mosaic.

Originality
Write a story about something that is orange and brown.

Elaboration
Draw a November picture using lots of orange and brown details.

Observation
Take a walk and look for things that are orange and brown.

HOW TO USE THE WORKSHEETS

TEACHING SUGGESTIONS

Following are suggestions for using each of the reproducible student worksheets that appear on pages 79–85. These are preceded by a management sheet you can use to record each child's activities.

Celebration Matrix (Originality)
Read a book about the first Thanksgiving, and then explain the worksheet by completing the first column with the entire class. Brainstorm possible answers for the other situations and have the children finish the assignment independently. This idea is easily adaptable as an interactive bulletin board or small group activity.

Past-Present-Future Associations (Flexibility)
Following a discussion of possible past, present, and future aspects of Thanksgiving, divide the class into small groups and encourage them to make unusual associations.

Thanksgiving Couplets (Originality)

As a class, list rhyming words for here, table, plate, and guests. Then practice rhyming patterns and possible endings for the couplets. Children complete the worksheet independently and may wish to illustrate their couplets.

Turkey Leftovers (Originality)

Have fun thinking of serious and fanciful ways to use turkey leftovers. Send this worksheet home as extension, or utilize the help of a parent volunteer. Children may wish to focus the recipe on family favorites or book characters' preferences.

Example:

Dad—mincemeat pie

Mom—cranberry sauce

Curious George—bananas

Snow White—applesauce

Pilgrim Puppet (Originality)

Use this pattern worksheet as a center activity. Allow time for interested students to organize a group presentation.

Thanksgiving Thoughts (Observation)

Encourage the skill of observation by exploring Thanksgiving thoughts through the five senses. As an extension, combine student ideas into a class poem or choral reading.

Home Project (Observation)

Send this worksheet home at the beginning of November. Assign an early enough "due date" to allow a follow-up discussion of family traditions.

Thanksgiving Management Sheet

Names	Celebration Matrix	Past-Present-Future	Thanksgiving Couplets	Turkey Leftovers	Pilgrim Puppet	Thanksgiving Thoughts	Home Project	

Celebration Matrix

Name _____

Imagine a Thanksgiving celebration that is...

	..."a reproduction of the first Thanksgiving..."	..."a celebration a turkey would enjoy..."	..."an international celebration..."	..."a celebration in space enroute to another galaxy..."	..."your idea..."
Who would be on your guest list?					
What would you include on the menu?					
What activities or games would you plan?					

Compare and contrast! How do your answers differ? Why?

PAST-PRESENT-FUTURE ASSOCIATIONS

Think of words that are associated with Thanksgiving celebrations of the...

...PAST...	...PRESENT...	...FUTURE
Pilgrim	microwave	space

Try some "forced comparisons"! Use two different words from the lists above... think of a way to associate the words.

Pilgrim	and microwave	→ they both work hard
	and	→
	and	→
	and	→
	and	→
	and	→
	and	→

THANKSGIVING COUPLETS

Thanksgiving is here,
A turkey feels _____ .

Dad is baking a
pumpkin pie.
When it's on the table,
I won't be _____ !

Look at my plate!
_____
_____

Here come the guests!
_____
_____

Now try
your own!

?!? TURKEY LEFTOVERS ?!?

Serious cooks: Experiment at home and bring in a sample of your creation!

Imaginative thinkers: Create a purely fanciful recipe with unusual ingredients!

From the kitchen of _____
                              student's name

_____
        name of recipe

Serves:

   Ingredients:

Procedure:

Check one: ☐ real recipe   ☐ imaginary recipe

Consider making the cookbook turkey-shaped!

Have the completed cookbook available for checkout.

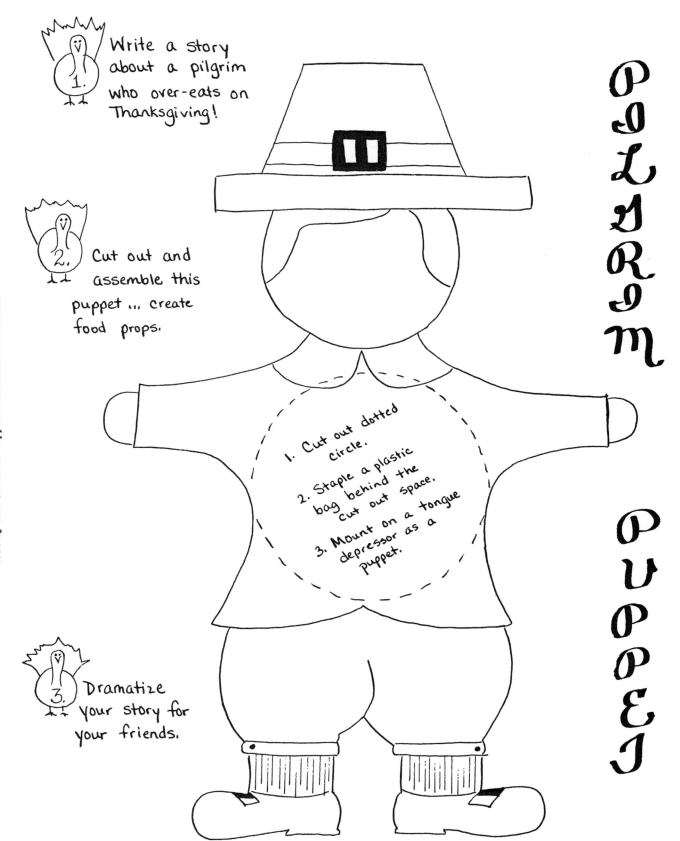

1. Write a story about a pilgrim who over-eats on Thanksgiving!

2. Cut out and assemble this puppet ... create food props.

3. Dramatize your story for your friends.

1. Cut out dotted circle.

2. Staple a plastic bag behind the cut out space.

3. Mount on a tongue depressor as a puppet.

PILGRIM

PUPPET

Name _____

Thanksgiving Thoughts...

I love to see ... _____
_____
_____

I enjoy the smells of... _____
_____
_____

My favorite tastes are... _____
_____
_____

Interesting textures include... _____
_____
_____

Sounds that make me happy are... _____
_____
_____
_____

Illustrate your answers in a poster, mobile or display.

Name _____

Due:

Who is going somewhere to visit?

Who has someone coming to visit?

Who has more than 10 dinner guests expected?

Who will have the same menu as last year's dinner?

Does anyone fix their pet a special meal?

Your idea -

HOME PROJECT

7. Compare and contrast with friends

6. Return to school

5. Complete graph

4. Tabulate information

3. Gather information

2. Read over with parents

1. Take home

List the people you consulted for your research:

Bulletin Board Ideas

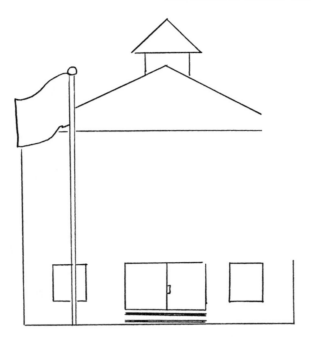

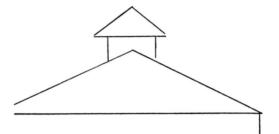

Enlarge the schoolhouse pattern. Post it in the center of a bulletin board. Research unusual facts about your school, record them on schoolhouse-shaped pieces of construction paper, and arrange them around the main schoolhouse.

© 1990 by The Center for Applied Research in Education

American Education Week

Consider all the things a pencil might tell someone about your school. Have students record their answers on pencil shapes . . . and arrange these around the bulletin board, too.

Finally, have each student write an elaborate description of your school. Share, compare, and tally all the different ideas. Combine the ideas into one long narrative printed on a sentence strip. Display it along the bottom of the bulletin board.

TURKEY TALES

Outline a bulletin board with November words your class brainstorms.

On chart paper, write a story with your class. Encourage students to use as many of the brainstormed words as they can. As you are writing, cover the words used from the list with turkey shapes.

Invite another class to figure out the missing words by using context clues.

The visiting class can then write a "turkey tale" for your class to solve.

Extensions: Allow interested students to write individual "turkey tales." Adapt the idea by changing the seasonal shape (instead of turkeys, use hearts, clouds, flowers, etc.).

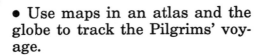

- Use maps in an atlas and the globe to track the Pilgrims' voyage.

- Sit and observe an activity in the library. What would a turkey have to say about it?

- Fill in a turkey shape with facts about turkeys. Post these feather activities and directions:

During independent work time, make tracks to the library to gobble up some of these activities. As each activity is complete, add feathers to the turkey on our bulletin board. Provide "feathers" for children to add to the turkey each time they complete an activity. Consider allowing interested students to work with a partner. Be sure to schedule time for students to share their products.

- Check for filmstrips or records related to Thanksgiving.

- Read a magazine article related to Thanksgiving.

- Look up turkeys. List their attributes. What other birds have each of the turkeys' attributes?

- Spend ten minutes on free reading!

- Compare different encyclopedia entries about Thanksgiving, Pilgrims, Indians, etc.

- Pilgrims had few books as personal possessions. Spend time in the library writing how you think they would feel about having so many books surround them.

- Count the number of books listed in the card catalog on Thanksgiving, Pilgrims, and Indians. List the titles and number of pages of each.

- Graph your data from the above activity.

- Write story problems using classmates' names and information from the graph.

PARENT CONNECTIONS

THANKSGIVING

Conduct a special show and tell after the holiday weekend by using a riddle format. Have students bring an object that represents something they did over the holiday weekend. They should conceal their objects in bags and have written clues ready! Post the clues, allow thinking time, then share! For a simpler version, have children give clues orally one at a time while the rest of the class guesses.

Send home a basic shape (square, rectangle, triangle, etc.) and ask children to create a turkey out of that shape using whatever materials they have on hand. When turkeys come back to school, set up a "Gobble, gobble, gobble" display.

Create a class book on the topic "Thankfulness." Have children add pictures, poems, and stories of things for which they are thankful. Check out the book overnight for students to share at home. Provide space in the back of the book for parents to add their own comments and thoughts. Start early so every home gets a chance to enjoy it!

Send home a worksheet eliciting Thanksgiving memories from families. Plan time for sharing, then have children write personal essays on Thanksgiving to take home and share over the holiday.

Start a bulletin board-sized collage of turkey illustrations. Encourage children to look through papers, magazines, coloring books, etc., to find *any* type of picture that depicts a turkey. Mount them around a realistic picture of a turkey. Initiate a class discussion of likenesses/differences and how the artists may have arrived at each turkey "character." Encourage children to draw their own imaginative turkey characters.

Send home a turkey outline on a plain piece of paper with instructions to list attributes of turkeys along the outline. Encourage family participation and research skills to generate a very long list of attributes. At school, compare attribute lists. Reward completion of the assignment, long lists (fluent thinking), unusual ideas (original thinking), and so on.

5

December Songs

TEACHING ACTIVITIES

INSTRUMENTS

Fluency

List all of the instruments you can recall. Find local musicians to interview.

Flexibility

What unusual sounds can you achieve using the same instrument?

Originality

Find something at home with which to create a unique rhythm instrument. Have a class rhythm band.

Elaboration

Write a story involving musical instruments.

Observation

In what kinds of places can you find musical instruments? Make a poster or graph to show your information.

SOUND EFFECTS

Fluency

List all the examples you can think of in which sound effects are used.

Flexibility

How do people and animals use sounds as signals?

Originality

Divide the students into groups and have children add sound effects to different stories. Have each group share its adapted version.

Elaboration

Build a sound train. The first person makes a sound, the second person repeats it and adds a new sound, the third person repeats the first two sounds and adds a new sound. Continue until each child has a chance to contribute!

Observation

Find a place to sit and listen. Record all the sounds that occur. Write a story that follows the sequence of the sounds you heard.

CREATIVE MOVEMENT

Fluency

Play different types of music and have a class movement show.

Flexibility

How many different ways can you move while standing or sitting in one spot?

Originality

Invent a specific movement or movement sequence. Name it!

Elaboration

Study a mime artist. Create an elaborate mime sketch of your own!

Observation

How is the way people move affected by their emotions?

BEETHOVEN'S BIRTHDAY

Fluency

Build an information base. Collect as many facts as you can about Beethoven.

Flexibility

If Beethoven came to visit your school, what would you show him?

Originality

What three questions would you ask Beethoven if you could meet him? What conversation might you have?

Elaboration

How would you celebrate Beethoven's birthday? Be sure to use facts from your information search. Example: Serve a "whole note" cake.

Observation

Conduct a survey to find what facts people can tell you about Beethoven. Graph the results.

HOW TO USE THE WORKSHEETS

TEACHING SUGGESTIONS

Following are suggestions for using each of the reproducible student worksheets on pages 94–97. These are preceded by a management sheet for recording each student's activities.

Note: For this set of worksheets, define the terms lyrics, rhythm, and composer with the class to ensure a common knowledge base. Consider enlisting the aid of the music teacher or a musically inclined parent volunteer.

Take a Look at Lyrics (Observation)

Develop an awareness of lyric comprehension through favorite seasonal songs. Provide a center with songsheets and taped versions of favorite songs. Children can read or listen to their favorite song as they complete this worksheet.

Musical Fill-Ins (Originality)

Sing "Jingle Bells" with the blank worksheet projected on the wall. Ask children to clap for every missing word. Brainstorm possibilities for the blanks and then have children complete the worksheet independently. Give opportunities for small groups or individuals to perform their adapted versions.

December Songfest (Fluency)

Ask children to complete this worksheet independently at the beginning of the month. Use it while planning special activities.

Song Settings (Elaboration)

Encourage students to consider what might have inspired a songwriter to compose a particular song. As children complete this worksheet, encourage use of detail in the illustrations.

December Songs Management Sheet

Names	Take a Look at Lyrics	Musical Fill-ins	December Songfest	Song Settings		

♫ Take A Look At Lyrics !

My favorite seasonal song is...
_____

List !

Who is the song about?

What is the song about?

Where does the song take place?

Consider! What is REAL in the song?
What is UNREAL in the song?
List your thoughts!

♫ REAL   UNREAL ♪

_____
Name

Musical Fill-Ins!

 Change the nouns in this favorite seasonal song... Share your new version with the class!

Jingle

Jingle _____, Jingle _____
Jingle all the way
Oh what fun it is to ride
In a _____

Dashing through the _____
In a _____
O'er the _____ we go
Laughing all the way!
_____ On _____ ring
Making _____ bright
What fun it is to laugh and sing
Our _____ song tonight!

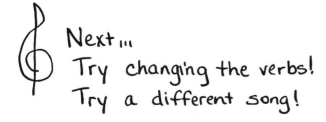

Next...
Try changing the verbs!
Try a different song!

Name _____

♫ December Songfest

List songs you'd like to sing in December ...

Put a ★ by a song you could teach to the class!

Name _____

♪ Song Settings

List two favorite songs...then draw scenes in which the songs may have been inspired!

Name

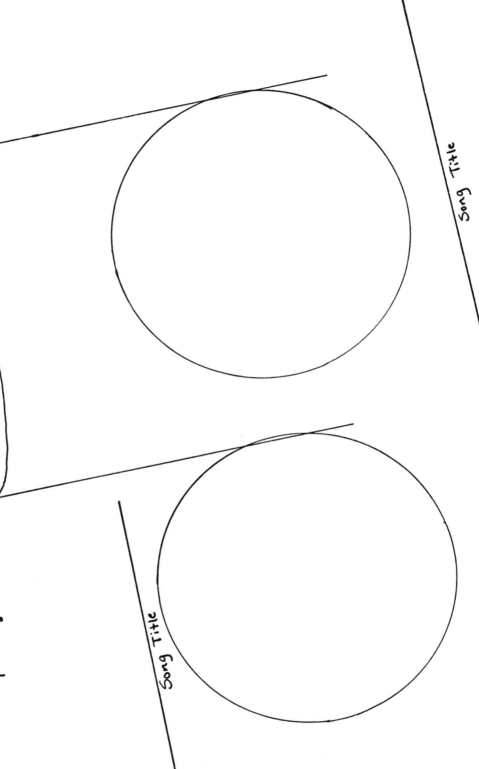

Song Title

Song Title

Bulletin Board Ideas
Think Twice

Woodwinds

Brass

Strings

Percussion

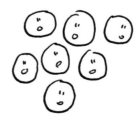

Use this bulletin board to promote flexible thinking. After introducing the different types of musical instruments, encourage students to think of alternative definitions of the groups. Have them illustrate their ideas and add them to the board.

That's Just My Style!

Invite children to bring in favorite musical selections of their own and of their parents. Play a "bit" of each and organize the titles of the songs under corresponding headings (e.g., Jazz, Classical, Pop, etc.)

Have the children print the song titles on large musical notes to post on a bulletin board. Consider playing different selections during independent work times!

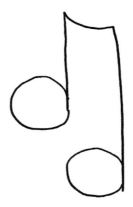

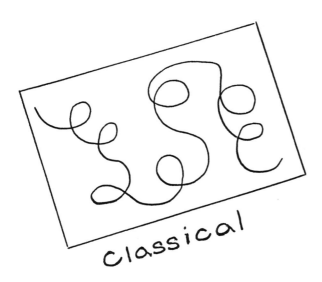

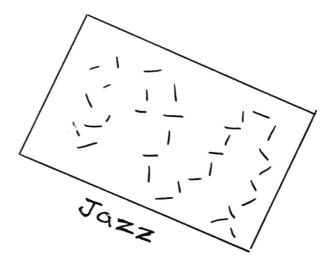

As an extension activity, draw while listening to different selections. What differences are in the pictures drawn to classical music as compared to those drawn to jazz music? Lullabies as compared to rock and roll?

PARENT CONNECTIONS

HOLIDAY MUSIC

Interview parents for song favorites. Find out which parents play musical instruments. Which parents played instruments as children?

Discuss or graph the different ways that families enjoy music.

6

Holiday Gifts

TEACHING ACTIVITIES

SURPRISES

Fluency

What are all the times when a surprise is appreciated?

Flexibility

How does a surprise feel to the person giving it? The person receiving it? The people watching?

Originality

Make up an original holiday—incorporate a surprise.

Elaboration

Write clues leading to a surprise for a friend to discover!

Observation

Notice facial expressions for different kinds of surprises. Make a book to show your observations.

FAVORITE ITEMS

Fluency

What special items do you see in use only in December?

Flexibility

If you were one of those items, how would you feel this month?

Originality

Compile stories (see Elaboration) into a family memories book. Share the book and then store it in a place where *it* will become a favorite item.

Elaboration

What is the "story" behind your favorite December item?

Observation

Survey your friends for their favorite items. Classify the items as toys, foods, ornaments, etc.

TOYS

Fluency

List all your toys and then classify them.

Flexibility

Research toys from different cultures. Adapt one toy as an American version.

Originality

Read a book about toys you can make. Use the information to invent a new toy.

Elaboration

Play with a forgotten toy. Give a long explanation of *why* you forgot it.

Observation

Compare toys for different age groups.

LIGHTS

Fluency

Make a flip book of all the different forms of light.

Flexibility

Write a description of Christmas from the point of view of the trees. What do they think of the holiday lights?

Write a description of Hanukkah from the point of view of a menorah. What does it think of the holiday lights?

Originality

Personalize a lampshade with decorative shapes.

Elaboration

Plan a puppet show with a friend. Incorporate spotlights!

Observation

Take note of unusual ways lights are used during the holidays.

BOXES

Fluency

What are all the different ways to stack your boxes?

Flexibility

Use a box to make a noisemaker for New Year's Eve.

Originality

Invent a game using different boxes.

Elaboration

Make an elaborate box puppet.

Observation

Analyze all the different ways in which boxes are used in your house.

HOW TO USE THE WORKSHEETS

TEACHING SUGGESTIONS

Following are suggestions for using each of the worksheets on pages 106–111. These are preceded by a management sheet you can use to record each child's activities.

Home Project (Fluency)

Send this worksheet home at the beginning of the month. Compile the family games/activities together into one booklet. Reproduce the booklet as a holiday gift for each family.

Present Perspectives (Flexibility)

Encourage a different point of view of the holidays by asking children to role play the thoughts of a present before it is opened. Use the worksheet as independent follow-up.

Wrap It Up (Fluency, Originality)

Accept unusual ideas as children think of a variety of gift wrappings. Compare their responses. What are the most unusual ideas?

Gift's Feelings (Elaboration)

In using this worksheet, encourage children to focus on supplying lots of interesting details in their descriptions. Role playing the situation before writing will generate increased detail.

Clue Me In (Observation)

Discuss the concept of "clues" using a teacher-prepared example. Then work through the process of writing clues. Children independently develop clues based on the five senses for gifts of their choice. They should check the clarity of their clues with a parent volunteer or buddy. Post completed worksheets on a bulletin board for everyone's enjoyment.

If Gifts Were Wishes (Originality)

Set the stage for this worksheet by discussing non-material gifts such as good wishes for other people. Have a parent volunteer take children's dictated responses, or have children respond independently. As an extension, make a class tape recording of their wishes.

Holiday Gifts Management Sheet

Names	Home Project	Present Perspectives	Wrap It Up	Gift's Feelings	Clue Me In	If Gifts Were Wishes	

Present Perspectives

Make a list of all the things you might see if you were a present sitting on a table.

On the back of this paper, draw what the room would look like from _your_ perspective.

Name _____

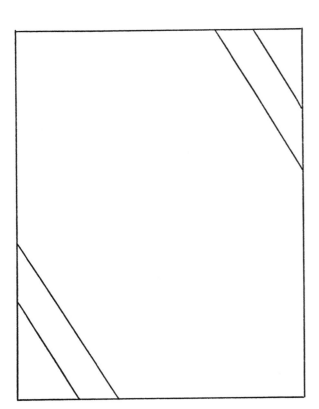

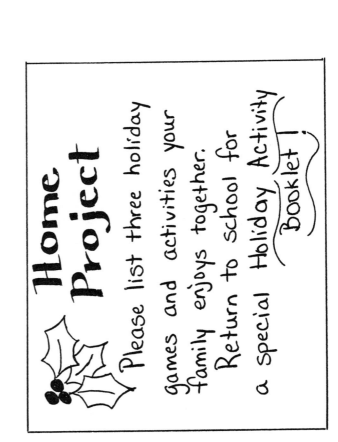

Home Project

Please list three holiday games and activities your family enjoys together. Return to school for a Special Holiday Activity Booklet!

Wrap It Up!

Newspaper...tissue paper...bandana...

Directions: Outline the drawing of the gift by making a list of all the different things you could use to wrap a gift.

Name _____

Name _____

Describe a gift's feelings as...

☐ it's being purchased

_____
_____
_____
_____
_____
_____
_____

☐ it's being wrapped

_____
_____
_____
_____
_____
_____

☐ it's waiting to be opened

_____
_____
_____
_____
_____
_____

☐ it's being opened

_____
_____
_____
_____
_____
_____

Name_____

dab of glue

1. Cut out the pictures. Glue them on the boxes so they flip up.
2. Draw something under the picture that could be wrapped inside the gift.
3. Write "five senses" clues!

dab of glue

It looks _____
It sounds _____
It feels _____
It smells _____
It tastes _____

It looks _____
It sounds _____
It feels _____
It smells _____
It tastes _____

dab of glue

CLUE ME IN

dab of glue

It looks _____
It sounds _____
It feels _____
It smells _____
It tastes _____

It looks _____
It sounds _____
It feels _____
It smells _____
It tastes _____

If Gifts Were Wishes,

what would your gifts be... and who would they be for?

_____
_____
_____
_____
_____
_____
_____
_____
_____
_____
_____
_____
_____
_____
_____
_____
_____
_____

_____
Name

Bulletin Board Ideas

SURPRISE!

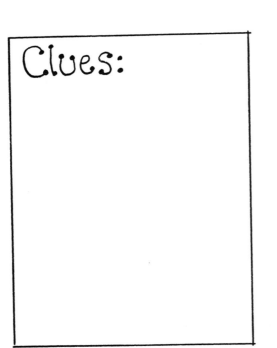

Clues:

Use this bulletin board idea as incentive during the month of December to encourage responsible behavior. Each day of the week post a clue related to a surprise planned for Friday. Give children an opportunity to guess... but don't reveal the surprise until Friday. How many children guessed correctly? Suggestions for surprises: a special filmstrip, a new picture book and free reading time, a penny and time to play a heads or tails game, art materials, etc.

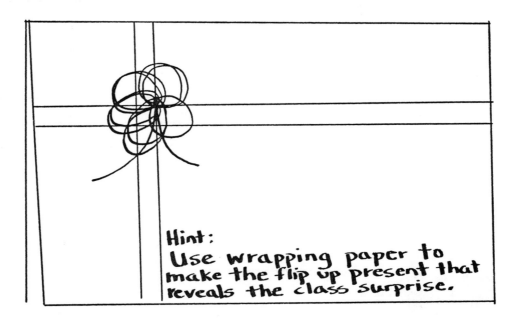

Hint:
Use wrapping paper to make the flip up present that reveals the class surprise.

Construct a "3-D" Jack-in-the-Box on a bulletin board and use this pattern for children's creative writing. Explore the following questions with children: What would you look like if you were a jack-in-the-box? How would it feel? What could pop out of your box that could surprise your friends? What's the most important thing you would want people to know about you?

After the warm-up discussion, write along with your class during a ten minute independent writing period. Instead of sharing their stories immediately, post them around the bulletin board and feature one each day by pinning it to the central jack-in-the-box's hands. Take time to read it aloud.

PARENT CONNECTIONS

GIFTS AND SURPRISES

Provide an assortment of story books and idea books to be checked out by students and their parents. Parent and child then plan a simple surprise (craft, cooking activity, art project, book sharing) for the class sometime during the month of December.

Children always enjoy making special surprises for their parents. Easy projects include:

- doorknob hangers
- sun catchers
- ornaments such as felt Christmas tree pins, bread dough decorations, stitched Christmas stockings that hold a special wish
- painted rock paperweight
- tile hot plate
- posterboard frame for a picture of the child taken at school

Decorate a medium-sized box for children to use as a "Winter Wonder Box of Sharing." Children can take turns taking the box home and bringing it back with something to share with the class—perhaps a special family book, a non-breakable holiday decoration, a collection of photographs, a recording or song, a painting, or a classroom treat.

Send home a note at the beginning of the month explaining the idea to parents, and tape the following letter to the inside of the box to serve as a log and reminder:

Dear Families,
This is our Winter Wonder Box of Sharing. It provides your child an opportunity to share something special from your home that relates to December and the many celebrations families enjoy. Please don't feel you must do something elaborate—favorite family stories, photos, decorations, treats, songs, thoughts, etc., are the focus. If you are uncomfortable sharing something from your home, just enclose a "winter wish" for our students. Happy thoughts are an important sharing too!

Be sure to write class thank-yous to families after the box has been to their home. Consider sharing something from *your* home too!

7

Christmas Creativity

TEACHING ACTIVITIES

BE A WORD WATCHER

Fluency

Replace all the "well worn" words in a favorite holiday story, poem, or song.

EXAMPLE: Rudolph, the crimson-muzzled Rangifertarandus.

Play with free associations of holiday words by listing each word students suggest as you go around the class.

Assign "word talks" as a home project. Children research a word, find as many examples of its use as possible, then present a "talk" about the word from an expert's point of view.

Flexibility

Brainstorm appropriate settings for a word's usage. Why would you not encounter the word elsewhere?

Originality

Play a "meaning madness" game in which students present one correct and two alternative definitions for some uncommon words. Classmates must try to identify the correct meaning.

Elaboration

Dramatize a new word through charades, puppetry, skits, etc.

Lead the class through a mental imagery of a particular word by giving an elaborate oral description. Then ask students to draw the word adding decorative details from your description and their own imaginations.

Observation

Listen for intriguing words in conversations, cultural contexts, advertisements, television programs, radio, songs, movies, and so on. Ask students, parents, and faculty members to suggest interesting words they know. Look for unusual words in stories, newspapers, menus, displays, posters, etc. Develop a dictionary of the most intriguing words.

EVERGREENS

Fluency

Make a class mural showing all kinds of evergreens. Focus on shapes, needles, patterns, etc. Note the "originality" idea designed to be added to your mural.

Flexibility

Consider alternative points of view. How are evergreens important to the forest? Forest inhabitants? Cities? The ocean? List responses on a chart.

Originality

Identify a favorite evergreen and write a poem about it. Share the poems by adding them to the evergreen mural.

Elaboration

Create an elaborately decorated tree for a favorite literary character. Include items especially suited for that character.

Observation

Research different types of evergreens. Use the information on an observation walk around the school grounds and neighborhood. How many different types can be found?

CELEBRATIONS

Fluency

What are all the types of celebrations people have? Make a bulletin board sized calendar for December and list student birthdays plus . . .

     ____ Hanukkah
   5th Walt Disney's birthday
   7th Pearl Harbor Day
  10th Human Rights Day
  16th Beethoven's birthday
  17th Wright Brothers' flight
   ____ Winter Solstice
  25th Christmas Day
  26th Boxing Day
  31st New Year's Day

Categorize the reasons for celebrations!

Flexibility

Stretch students' thinking by asking for examples of other ways to remember and commemorate events. Consider monuments, greeting cards, picture albums, etc. Build an idea around each form of celebration. Construct a monument to "recess," design lunch time greeting cards, design a bulletin board to commemorate your class, etc.

Originality

Refer to the bulletin board calendar (see Fluency). Brainstorm with the class ideas for celebrations for each day that is blank. Organize committees to plan special activities for days such as "Favorite Class Book Day," "Art Day," "Warm-up Suits Day," "Most Popular Lunch Day," "Backwards Day," etc.

Elaboration

Challenge pairs of students to create an elaborate poster about one of the December celebrations. Examine various advertising brochures before doing the posters to note eye-catching techniques. Send the completed posters to another class and invite them to join you in the fun!

Observation

As your class enjoys the variety of December celebrations, appoint class members to take pictures and make note of people's reactions to the special events. Encourage the recorders to try different views of the festivities. For example, draw a picture of the day as viewed through binoculars, or summarize the day in one picture.

MILLICENT MOUSE

Here's an easy form of creative dramatics! Assign the following parts to three groups of students. Read the story and pause as they add sound effects each time their character is mentioned.

Teacher: say "shh, shh, shh"
Class: say "whisper, whisper, whisper"
Millicent Mouse: say "squeak, squeak, squeak"

A bell rang and the teacher welcomed her excited <u>class</u> on the last day before winter break. The <u>class</u> settled restlessly into their seats. As the <u>teacher</u> explained the morning work, the <u>class</u> thought of the holiday to come. Little did they know that they had an observer hiding behind the radiator. <u>Millicent Mouse</u> was wondering why everyone was so itchy! Even the <u>teacher</u> seemed preoccupied. <u>Millicent Mouse</u> was disappointed because she was learning to read with the class, and neither the <u>teacher</u> nor the <u>class</u> was following the routine!

As the day wore on, the <u>class</u> and the <u>teacher</u> became more excited. With the arrival of party goodies, <u>Millicent Mouse</u> sadly realized there would be no reading that day. In the midst of the gaiety, a paper slipped from a student's desk and bumped <u>Millicent Mouse</u> as it slid under the radiator. "What's this?" wondered <u>Millicent Mouse</u>. "Why, it has words . . ." and she proceeded to read that the <u>class</u> and the <u>teacher</u> would return in two weeks from a winter break.

At first <u>Millicent Mouse</u> was sad to know she'd be alone for two weeks. But then she realized . . . she had read the notice! And she knew that reading would continue when the <u>teacher</u> and the <u>class</u> returned. In the meantime, there were lots of yummy crumbs left over from the party, and <u>Millicent Mouse</u> happily munched on them as the <u>teacher</u> and the <u>class</u> left for their winter break.

MILLICENT MOUSE EXTENSIONS

Fluency

What other characters could be in the story?

Flexibility

Adapt the story to a different time of year.

Originality

Write a sequel to the story. What happens after the winter break? What adventures does Millicent Mouse have now that she knows how to read?

Elaboration

Add in other sound effects to the story.

Observation

What statements can you make about Millicent Mouse? Examples: She cares about reading. She notices lots of things.

HOW TO USE THE WORKSHEETS

TEACHING SUGGESTIONS

Following are suggestions for using the reproducible worksheets on pages 122–126. These are preceded by a management sheet for recording children's activities.

Santa's Sleigh (Originality)

Brainstorm different toys in Santa's bag and what talent each toy would have (example: Jack-in-the-Box could jump on the rooftop). After writing an independent story, some children may wish to illustrate or dramatize their story.

Santa's Reindeer (Fluency)

Discuss the imaginary nature of Santa's reindeer and the possible origins of their names. Cite unusual name resources such as the dictionary, globe, etc. Encourage children to be thoughtful of why they would choose a particular name for a reindeer as they complete this worksheet.

December Descriptions (Observation)

Read the worksheet with the class. Discuss one of the comparison stems. Encourage a variety of responses. As children complete the other examples independently, encourage more than one response for each description. Compile all the ideas into a class Santa-shaped book.

Santa's "To Do" List (Flexibility)

List Santa's tasks in getting ready for the holiday by allowing children to work with buddies, a small group, or with their family. As an extension, consider writing a list for different Christmas characters such as Mrs. Santa Claus, Rudolph, etc. Copy the ideas onto a large "To Do" list for the bulletin board.

Santa's Journal (Elaboration)

Discuss journals—why and how people write them. Children can write a detailed entry for four dates from Santa's point of view. They may want to vary the seasons of the entries or make the entries consecutive.

Christmas Creativity Management Sheet

Names	Santa's Sleigh	Santa's Reindeer	December Descriptions	Santa's "To Do" List	Santa's Journal

Santa's sleigh is broken... how could his bag of toys help him make his deliveries?

Santa's Sleigh

Santa's Reindeer

What are all the names you can think of for Santa's reindeer?

List them! Try to fill in the reindeer shape!

Name _____

December

Descriptions

Think of unusual things to complete these comparisons.

example:
His beard is as fluffy as a soufflé!

His eyes twinkle like _____

His belly shakes like _____

His suit is as red as _____

His beard is as fluffy as _____

His boots are as shiny as _____

Name _____

Santa's "To Do" List

Consider what Santa does during the year! Write a "to do" list for him.

Name:

Santa's Journal

_____
Name

_____
date

_____
date

_____
date

_____
date

Bulletin Board Ideas
Gingerbread Delights

Make December a Gingerbread Month in your classroom. Begin by having every child help in decorating a large gingerbread house. Then reproduce the pattern below and provide a variety of materials (sequins, rick-rack, glitter, etc.) for children to use in decorating their own individual gingerbread cookie. Arrange the cookies around the house. Read the story *The Gingerbread Man* or show a filmstrip of the story.

As extension, consider . . .

- writing different endings to the story and posting them on the board
- making individual gingerbread houses with milk cartons and graham crackers
- baking real gingerbread men
- paper folding gingerbread men to list short vowel words, long vowel words, synonyms, math problems, etc.
- telling a group holiday story by passing around a gingerbread doll . . . as each child holds the doll, he/she adds a sentence to the story
- creating salt-dough gingerbread men ornaments
- telling the story of *The Gingerbread Man* from one of the other characters' point of view

Holiday Sharing

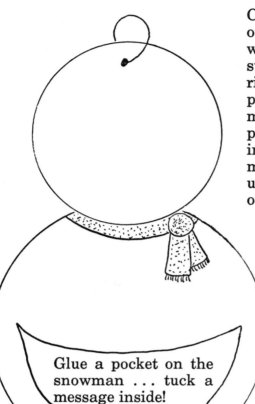

Create these holiday ornaments to share with someone else! Ask students to compose riddles, poems, math problems, stories, memories, etc. Incorporate the writings into one of these ornament designs . . . or use an idea of their own!

Glue a pocket on the snowman . . . tuck a message inside!

Double cut this ornament . . . flip up to write inside.

Double cut the bell, glue the edges. Insert the inside piece, pull down to see answer.

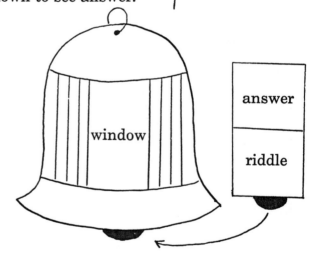

Gingerbread House Milk Carton . . . tuck the poem inside.

Double cut the package . . . slit to make windows that fold out. Write inside on the back piece.

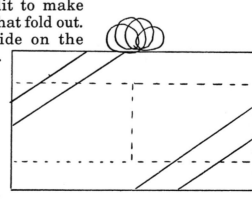

PARENT CONNECTIONS

CHRISTMAS CREATIVITY

Send home a 4″ x 6″ blank index card and a fine line marker for families to create a detailed illustration of favorite family traditions. When the cards are returned to school, invite students to share their illustrations and staple them together to form a chain.

Enjoy a holiday show and tell. Have students share something special from home that they look forward to seeing each December.

Use holiday cards to tell a picture story, or to make a collage or a mobile.

Ask students to list their favorite words on a construction paper frame. Use tissue paper to create a scene appropriate for those words by ironing the paper between sheets of waxed paper. Glue the scene between two frames to make a suncatcher of words. Hang it in the window!

8

Winter Weather

TEACHING ACTIVITIES

COMBINE CREATIVITY AND TRADE BOOKS

Fluency

List alternative titles for stories.

List titles for sequels to popular stories.

Publish a list of "Reader's Favorites" with short summaries of the stories.

Flexibility

If you were the author, what would you have to know to write the book?

Change the time, setting, or characters in a story. Summarize how it affects the outcome of the story.

Design a line of school supplies that uses a book as its theme.

Originality

Take the role of a book character. Meet with another book character and plan a play activity together.

Narrate different endings to the story.

Make elaborate book jackets, bookmarks, posters, mobiles, advertisements, puppets, cartoons, etc., to showcase your book.

Elaboration

Give an elaborate description of the book in just three minutes.

Choose one element of the story (setting, character, plot) and illustrate it with elaborate details.

Make a set of sequence cards for a story. Shuffle them and arrange them in a new order. Write a new story following that sequence. Add details for transitions.

Observation

Collect "artifacts" that represent the story.

Compare. How is this book like others you have read? Describe how a particular book character is like or unlike someone you know.

ICE

Fluency

Where are all the places you find ice?

Flexibility

What are all the words that have "ice" in them (nice, suffice, etc.)?

Originality

Find out about ice sculptures. Try your hand at it!

Elaboration

Pretend you are an ice cube. How does it feel? Describe your life.

Observation

Survey! Who prefers a drink with ice rather than without ice? Graph the information. Do experiments with ice. For example, what's the quickest way to melt ice?

CREATIVITY INDOORS

Fluency

Ask children to list all the indoor games they've played. Graph the results. Sponsor an "Indoor Games Day" during which everyone shares a favorite indoor game.

Flexibility

Challenge children to consider how they can use the classroom furniture and equipment to arrange an obstacle course. Have them present their ideas on a map of the classroom . . . take time to enjoy their obstacle course ideas!

Originality

Have children brainstorm adjectives about their favorite indoor places. Each child combines the adjectives into a poem and writes the poem on a poster picturing his/her special spot.

Elaboration

Take a walking tour of the school and enjoy noticing the outdoor scenes associated with each window. Ask children to write an elaborate description of one of the scenes. Can friends identify the matching window?

Observation

Post the following questions:

> . . . What indoor things can be done outdoors? How does that change the activity?
>
> . . . What outdoor things can be done indoors? How does that change the activity?

Compile children's thoughts into an indoors/outdoors class book. Illustrate the opposing settings for the same activity on opposite pages or at the top and bottom of each page.

CALENDAR CAPERS

Fluency

List all the people who use calendars. Identify the different types of calendars they use. Note why the calendar suits their particular needs.

Flexibility

In what ways do people keep track of the time and events without the use of a calendar?

Compile ideas into a book shaped like an elephant (remember that elephants have great memories).

Originality

Design a calendar for a specific person, occupation, or animal. Think about important events that should be noted throughout. Include details in the design that make it a personalized calendar.

Elaboration

Write a sales pitch or design an advertisement for a favorite calendar style. Discuss the economics of marketing a product. Provide tokens, model buying and selling, then let children role play a class sales convention.

Observation

Use a calendar to make note of various observations—weather, diet, exercise, correspondence, favorite event of the day, books read, and so on. Periodically look back to draw conclusions and make generalizations about the listings.

TAKE A LETTER . . . AND . . .

Fluency

Enjoy writing letters in a variety of formats: puzzle letters, "tab" letters (pull a tab to remove the letter from the envelope), pop-up cards, flip letters (each page is a different length for ease in flipping), photo essay letters, code letters, scroll letters, or even invisible ink letters.

Flexibility

Vary the writing instruments. Give students markers, colored pencils, felt-tip pens, crayons, chalk, paint, calligraphy pens, twigs and ink, cotton swabs and tempera paint, etc.

Mix letter writing with art projects: try a cube letter, a mobile letter, a letter in a painting, a poster letter, or a puppet letter.

Originality

Design your own stationery with shapes specific to the school, seasonal ideas, or a topic currently being studied.

Elaboration

Send letters in a shaped envelope, a cardboard tube, a decorated milk carton, or a treasure chest.

Observation

Ask children to monitor their mail at home for one week. What kinds of things are delivered? Have students categorize, compare with classmates, and make observations about their mail. What things did the children expect? What things were unexpected?

HOW TO USE THE WORKSHEETS

TEACHING SUGGESTIONS

Following are suggestions for using the reproducible worksheets on pages 136–140. These are preceded by a "Winter Weather Management Sheet" to help you keep track of each child's activities.

Weather Watch (Observation)

Conduct a discussion about feelings and how people show their feelings. Introduce weather as a "cause" for certain feelings. As a class, watch behavior for a day and discuss how the weather may have affected people.

Weather Class Book (Flexibility)

Children enjoy doing lots of things in lots of different kinds of weather. Use this worksheet to create a class book of weather activities. Then have fun "mis-matching" activities and weather to spark humorous stories.

Weather Web (Fluency)

Webbing is a written brainstorming technique. Model generating ideas to go with one branch of the web with the class. Let children branch off the other subtopics independently.

Weather Titles (Elaboration)

After using this worksheet to generate consequences, encourage children to develop the ideas into a story or their own weather titles.

Weather Writings (Flexibility)

Try this association exercise with a weather words list as a resource. Work through an example with the entire class, then use the worksheet as independent follow-up or as a center activity.

Winter Weather Management Sheet

Names	Weather Writings	Weather Class Book	Weather Web	Weather Titles	Weather Poem	

Weather Writings

Begin with a weather word and let your thoughts lead you into a free-verse poem. One word leads to the next until you've wound your way back to the original word.

Example:

rain
|
drops - splatter - umbrella - rain

Name _____

Weather Class Book

Teachers: Use this worksheet to make a class book. Each child illustrates a type of weather and activity that matches that weather. After pages are assembled, cut along the middle to create an opportunity to mix and match. Encourage students to then write about humorous mis-matches! example: Snow - using an umbrella

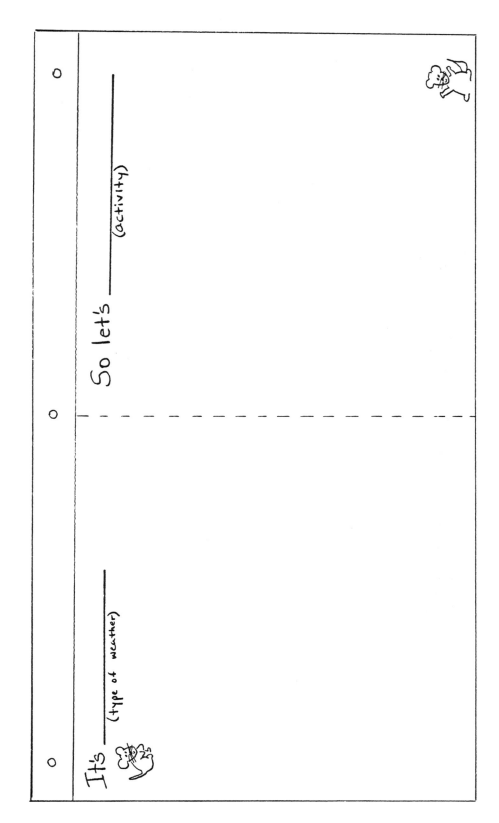

It's _____
(type of weather)

So let's _____
(activity)

Weather Web

_____
Name

A webbing is an outline form used to generate ideas related to a topic. Add bubbles as ideas are listed that are associated with a given topic.

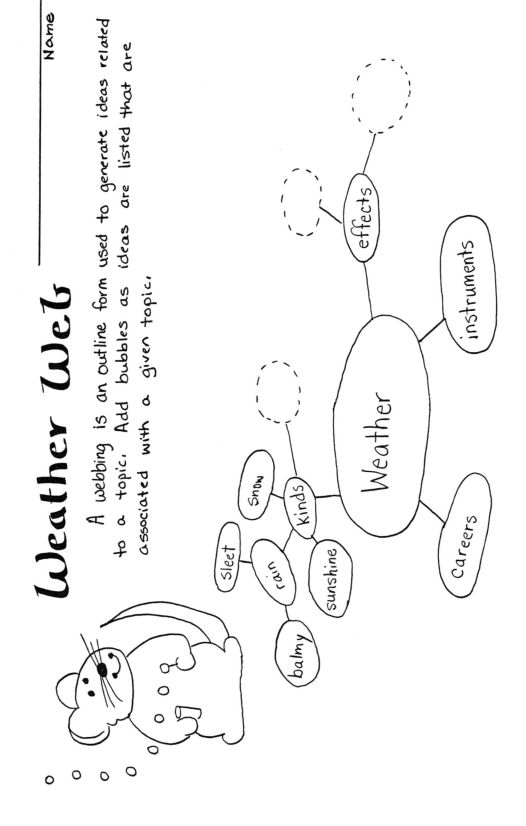

Organize a report from your webbing.

Weather Titles

Consider these titles ... list as many consequences for each that you can think of.

The Day the Storm HIT

The Sunniest Day Ever

A Weird Week of Weather

Sun.	Mon.	Tues.	Wed.	Thurs.	Fri.	Sat.

Name

Develop one of these titles/consequences into a story.

Weather Poem ...

How does weather affect people's behavior? Watch the people around you on days with different types of weather. Record your observations. Draw conclusions and write a humorous poem.

Name_____

Bulletin Board Ideas
BUDDY UP WITH BOOKS

Utilize January indoor time to promote silent reading. Sponsor a "buddy" reading club that integrates home reading time with school discussions and projects.

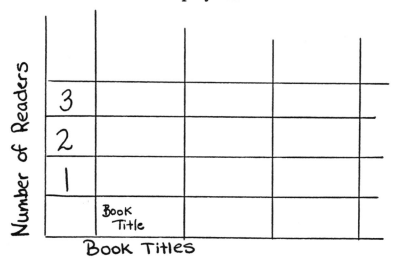

Compile a list of books that have been written in a series that are appropriate for the age level and interest level of your students. Send the list home. Children should choose a book to begin reading with a buddy and should keep track of their reading through a log that parents sign. As children finish a book, they color in a corresponding square on a graph to show how many children have read each book in the series.

When a group of children has finished the same book, a classroom discussion is held to interest others in the book.

At the end of the month, when all children have read as many of the books in the series as possible, plan a class book party. Enjoy cakes or cookies that are decorated with something special from the books read. As an activity during the party, have everyone complete a book project.

MY READING RECORD

Book Title: _____
            (Parent Signature)

Book Title: _____
            (Parent Signature)

Book Title: _____
            (Parent Signature)

            Name:

January Giant

Encourage children to develop responsibility at home during January by initiating a class project of carrying out specific tasks at home that will build a "January Giant."

Decide upon the tasks you'd like to emphasize with your class. Prepare a slip like the one below listing each task. Explain to the class that as they complete a task each day they should check the matching box. They try to practice as many things as possible each day. At the end of the week, they bring the slip back to school. Tally the number of checks each child has and pass out the same number of construction paper squares for the child to glue onto the giant (1 check = 1 square).

As children earn construction paper squares, the giant fills up in a mosaic pattern!

	Monday	Tuesday	Wednesday	Thursday	Friday
1.					
2.					
3.					
4.					
5.					
Other:					

© 1990 by The Center for Applied Research in Education

Send a letter home with the first slip explaining the goals and tasks to the parents. Each week give the students a new slip. Rather than set a required number of "checks," simply verbally reinforce those children who participate. Each week participation will grow as children watch each other glue squares to the giant.

Snow Wonder

Post the words SNOW WONDER in the middle of the bulletin board. Print the following questions on tissue paper snowflakes, and provide students with copies of the answer sheet snowflake below. Encourage them to reply to each snowflake question. As they do, post their snowflake close to the question to build a bulletin board of snowflakes!

- Did you ever wonder where you could water-ski in January? Which place would *you* choose to visit? Why?
- What snow beings could you make instead of snowmen?
- What could you use to create unusual tracks in the snow?
- What are all the hot drinks you could enjoy on a cold day?
- What would you plan for a winter picnic?
- What are all the ways to wrap a scarf around your neck?
- What would you plan for a winter block party?
- What sounds do you hear on a snowy day?

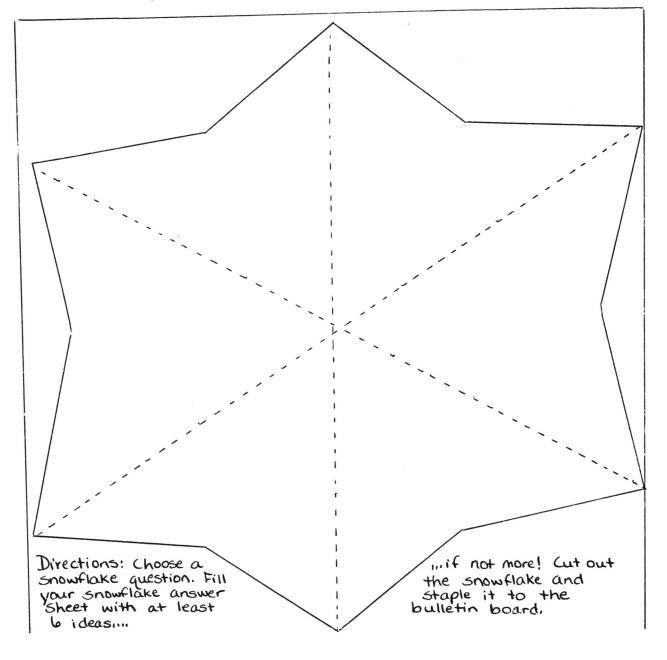

Directions: Choose a snowflake question. Fill your snowflake answer sheet with at least 6 ideas....

...if not more! Cut out the snowflake and staple it to the bulletin board.

PARENT CONNECTIONS

WINTER

Discuss the idea of resolutions with your parents. Compose together a resolution . . .

> you *want* to make,
> you *should* make,
> for a friend,
> for your teacher,
> for the President of the United States.

Talk with your family about where you would like to vacation in the wintertime. At school, make a graph to show how many families discussed warm places and how many discussed cold places.

Visit the library with your parents. Look for books about animal habits, tracks, etc., in winter. Keep a log of animals you notice this month.

9

Valentine Activities

TEACHING ACTIVITIES

FAMOUS AMERICANS

Fluency

Make a list of *all* the famous Americans you know. Why are they famous? Classify them.

Flexibility

Imagine you have a famous parent. What do you think life would be like? Write a personal essay about your family and family events.

Originality

Create an interactive bulletin board that displays famous Americans and outstanding characteristics of those famous Americans for your students to match. Mix both past and current famous Americans. Research to assist with identifying some distinguishing characteristics. Encourage interested students to add facts.

Elaboration

Start a scrapbook of present-day famous Americans. Search newspapers and magazines for information. Check with the librarian about other information sources.

Observation

What are some symbols that could represent some famous Americans? Design a badge or coat of arms for your favorite famous American.

HAPPY, DELIGHTED, GLAD . . .

Fluency

List all the synonyms for happy, and discuss their precise meanings or connotations. Turn the ideas into a "happy book" . . .

I'm _____ when _____

Flexibility

Encourage children to take a different point of view by considering someone else's happiness. For instance, what things could they do to relieve their parents' routines? Ask children to choose five things to do for their parents during the week of Valentine's Day. Write the tasks on heart coupons to present to Mom and Dad.

Originality

Use fabric crayons to create a T-shirt design about happiness. Iron the designs on T-shirts brought from home. (Dad's T-shirts make great sleep shirts!) Children might want to wear their happiness shirts to the class Valentine's party.

Elaboration

Brainstorm a list of songs about happiness. Which ones can the class sing? Excerpt single lines from each song to create a class medley. Elaborate with motions.

Observation

Create a boardgame of school happiness by observing various people around the school building. Make note of what pleases teachers, custodians, specialists, principals, etc. Build the ideas into a game in which the cards give happy situations and point values. The players read the cards and move that number of spaces. Or, players can move one space at a time and keep a tally of their points.

LIGHT AND SHADOW

Fluency

List things that are fun to do in lots of light. List things that require shadows. Compile your ideas in a book of "Contrasting Activities."

Start a collection of "light" phrases. For example, "you're the light of my life!"

Flexibility

Have fun creating shadow puppets, a shadow box, or a light show. Consider how shadows would look if they were a spectrum of color. Draw a picture in which there are "rainbow shadows."

Originality

Consider how light and shadow affect animal habits. Write a news report about your findings.

Use the dictionary. Make a poster showing all the definitions for the word "light."

Elaboration

Write a descriptive poem:

> Light is like . . .
> Night is like . . .
>
> In the daytime I like to
>   see. . .hear. . .touch. . .smell. . .
> In the nighttime I like to
>   see. . .hear. . .touch. . .smell. . .

Observation

Buddy up with a friend and trace each other's shadows on the sidewalk at different times during the day. Be sure to stay in the same spot for each tracing. What conclusions can you make from comparing the shadows?

Identify different light sources. What difference does that make in a shadow?

Visit an art display and notice how artists use light and shadow in their work. Can you tell where the light is coming from in paintings? Which part of the scene has lighter colors? How do shadows enhance the picture?

GROUNDHOGS

Fluency

Think of superstitions associated with different months.

Flexibility

What other compound words have "ground" and "hog" in them?

Originality

Write about a groundhog on a groundhog shadow shape.

Elaboration

Make a clay groundhog in a model of its habitat.

Observation

List a groundhog's attributes. What other things have each attribute? Make a chart to show your ideas.

OUR COUNTRY

Fluency

Interview friends and adults to collect a long list of facts about our country. Display the facts on a patriotic banner.

Flexibility

Locate our country on a variety of maps and globes.

Originality

Do something with red, white, and blue (e.g., a red, white, and blue pizza, a red, white, and blue playhouse).

Elaboration

Plan an elaborate All-American meal.

Observation

Draw or find pictures of patriotic symbols of our country.

HOW TO USE THE WORKSHEETS

TEACHING SUGGESTIONS

Following are suggestions for using the reproducible worksheets on pages 151–155. These are preceded by a "Valentine Activities Management Sheet" for use in individual recordkeeping.

A Message for You (Fluency, Flexibility)

Collect old valentines from class members and analyze the messages. Use this worksheet to encourage children to create their own unusual messages. For very interested students, allow opportunities for valentine card production.

Heart Codes (Elaboration)

Everyone loves codes! Try this versatile worksheet as an independent assignment, a buddy activity, a center activity, or a home project.

Care . . . and Share (Elaboration)

Discuss all the ways people show they care. Use this worksheet as a follow-up and provide time for discussing the observations. Graphing results is a possible extension for individuals or committees.

Valentine Village (Originality)

Imagine a heart-shaped village! Use this worksheet as a design sheet, then provide materials to interested students for actual construction.

Valentine Signatures (Observation)

Children enjoy collecting things. Schedule time for classmates to collect signatures on this worksheet—one signature per heart. Try to get lots of different people to sign. Consider out-of-class time for collecting signatures, too. Blank hearts may be filled in with original ideas for signatures.

Valentine Activities Management Sheet

Names	A Message for You	Heart Codes	Care . . . and Share	Valentine Village	Valentine Signatures

Name_____

A Message for You

Try some unusual messages...

Can you think of other animals and/or messages?

No hibernating allowed...
Be My Valentine!

There's nothing fishy about this message...
Be My Valentine!

Send messages in heart codes...

Create a different design for each ♡.
Compose a message for a friend
to decode.

Extension: Cut the designs into linoleum, potatoes
or styrofoam ... and <u>print</u> your
message.

Name _____

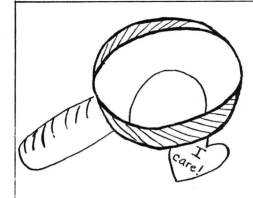

Care...
and Share

Observe friends and family.
List the things you see
happening that show caring.

Caring for People	Caring for Animals	Caring for Things

Name

Make a
Valentine Village!

Use heart-shapes to create an entire village -
buildings, landscape, occupants, signs!

Welcome to
Valentine
Village!

Name _____

Valentine Signatures

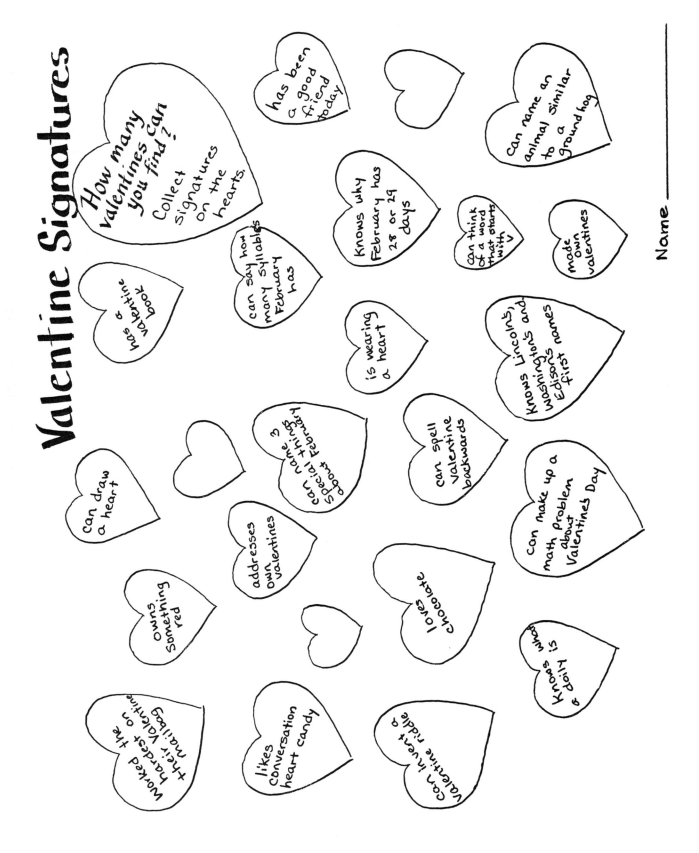

How many valentines can you find? Collect signatures on the hearts.

has been a good friend today

can name an animal similar to a groundhog

knows why February has 28 or 29 days

can think of a word that starts with V

made own valentines

has a valentine book

can say how many syllables February has

is wearing a heart

knows Lincoln's, Washington's and Edison's first names

can draw a heart

can name 3 special things about February

can spell valentine backwards

can make up a math problem about Valentines Day

addresses own valentines

owns something red

loves chocolate

knows what a heart is doing

worked the hardest on their Valentine mailbag

likes conversation heart candy

can invent a valentine riddle

Name _____

Bulletin Board Ideas
Shadowing!

Will the groundhog see his shadow? Have children vote Yes or No by writing their names under the appropriate column.

Yes   No

What will the groundhog say when he wakes up this year?

Cut shadows out of black construction paper . . . ask children to respond to the above question by writing on the shape with chalk.

Give the same task to colleagues . . . collect everyone's response and display them on a bulletin board.

Bulletin Board-Sized Code

Reproduce 26 hearts from the shape below. Ask each child in your room to decorate one in a simple manner. Collect hearts and display each one next to a letter of the alphabet. Challenge children to "code" messages, display them, and allow others free time to solve them.

PARENT CONNECTIONS

FEBRUARY

Start a family valentine at school by having children illustrate their family and complete the following (adapt it if necessary):

My family is _____ ! Everyone is special—Mom, Dad, Brother, Sister, Me . . .

We have fun when _____ .

Our favorite family picture is _____ because _____
_____ .

Things we always do that are special are _____
_____ .

Send home a square of white material on which parents and their children stitch a simple design of something that brings them happiness. Children bring their completed square back to school to be put into a large class quilt all about happiness.

Try these February wake-up ideas:

- Ask students to keep a chart of when everyone in their home wakes up. Interview family members for reasons *why* they wake up! Take time to share the results and compile ideas into a humorous class book entitled *Sure-Fire Wake-Up Ideas*.
- Devote a library visit to finding short books that would be easy and quick to share. Have students take turns sharing the books at home during "Breakfast Book Time." Attach a comment sheet to each book so families can jot down their favorite part of the story.

10

Friendship

TEACHING ACTIVITIES

VISITING

Fluency
Plan for a friend's visit. List all the things you plan to do.

Flexibility
Brighten someone's day with a visit. What can you do for them?

Originality
Write about an imaginary visit.

Elaboration
Research famous visits (moon landing, political meetings, Little Red Riding Hood, etc). Compile a booklet.

Observation
Visit a local park. Enjoy time outside, and keep a log of your observations.

TWOS-DAY ACTIVITIES

Buddy children up in "twos" to enjoy these activities on the second schoolday of the week.

Fluency

Make a long list of rhyming words. Let one partner write a line for a couplet and give it to the other partner to complete.

Flexibility

Choose a topic. Find pictures in magazines to go with your topic. Can a classmate guess your topic by looking at your picture collection? Can he/she give a verbal example of something else that would go with your topic?

Have students hold a scarf between them for the entire play period. Whatever they do must be done together!

Originality

Ask partners to create a stitchery design between them. Stitch all partners' squares into a wall hanging to donate to the school.

Have partners read plain-backed books from the library and then have them create colorful book jackets. Laminate the jackets and use them on the books to perk up the bookshelves and student interest!

Elaboration

Have partners adapt a short story into a play, then read it out loud using different disguised voices.

Observation

Partners go on a tour of the school and make a list of sighted words they both can read. Put one of these words on each page of a book and illustrate the words.

Notice "hour activities." List school helpers in your building. Every hour, check to see what they are doing. Note the time and illustrate their activity. Put illustrations on a poster that features a clock with moveable hands.

CELEBRATE FRIENDSHIP

Fluency

Use wrapping paper for a bulletin board background and have students write friendly thoughts on heart shapes. As students share friendship thoughts, encourage use of synonyms for the word "friend" (pal, buddy, amigo, etc.). Watch the friendly messages increase by leaving blank hearts nearby for children to fill in during spare moments.

Flexibility

An interesting "turn-around" question for February is . . .

When might you need a friend, and when might a friend need you? Have children dramatize the situations they think of in puppet shows or skits.

Originality

Write a poem about friendship. Display it on a poster of hearts, in a book of friendly illustrations, or written with fabric crayons and ironed on a banner.

Elaboration

Brainstorm all the words you can think of that are associated with friendship. Use the list to create concrete poems about friendship.

On silhouettes of classmates, write adjectives of friendship and display them.

Observation

Friendship is readily noticed among people, but what about animals? How do we know animals have friends? Challenge children to write stories about animal friendships.

Use an instant camera to snap photos of friendship during the day. Compile them into a photo essay on friendship.

EXTENSIONS FOR FRIENDSHIP BOOKS

Compile a class collection of books that tell stories about friendships. After sharing them, enjoy these activities.

Fluency

What are all the things the characters do to show they are friends?

Flexibility

Take the author's point of view . . . what may have inspired the story?

Originality

Add a chapter or event to the book that describes a new aspect of the characters' friendship.

Elaboration

Take one event in the story and explain it in great detail.

Observation

Write facts about the story on an appropriate shape. (For example, use an elephant shape to write facts about Babar.)

HOW TO USE THE WORKSHEETS

TEACHING SUGGESTIONS

Following are suggestions for using the reproducible worksheets on pages 164–168. These are preceded by a "Friendship Management Sheet" for use in recordkeeping.

Friendship Means (Originality)

Brainstorm friendship words. Demonstrate how to complete the poem. Show that words can fit across the FRIENDSHIP stem by matching beginning sounds, middle sounds, or ending sounds. After doing a few examples together, children complete the worksheet independently. This strategy is easily adaptable to other words and topics.

Friends Are Fun (Observation)

In using this worksheet, encourage children to consider several answers for each sentence stem instead of just recording their first thought. Encourage students to stretch beyond the common responses such as "nice" and "good."

Friendship Word Chain (Flexibility)

Discuss the word chain with the class. Consider using this worksheet as an oral exercise or small group activity. Brainstorm other friendship words before having students create an original word chain.

Animal Friendship (Originality)

Animal friendships may be between two or more animals or between animals and people. Encourage children to think of an unusual friendship before writing their story. Consider factual stories as well as fictional. Enlarge the patterns to create shape books of the stories.

Friendship Puppet Show (Elaboration)

Use this worksheet to help children plan a puppet show. Have a parent volunteer guide children in developing and incorporating details such as puppet interaction, scenery, props, and so on.

Friendship Management Sheet

Names	Friendship Means	Friends Are Fun	Friendship Word Chain	Animal Friendship	Friendship Puppet Show

Friendship
Means...

F
R
I
E
N
D
S
H
I
P

Think of words that go with friendship - fit them
horizontally into the word poem above. Illustrate!
example: laugHter

A *Friendship Book* ... Complete the sentences and illustrate. Cut along the dotted lines. Tape in a long accordion-strip fold to make a book.

Friends Are Fun!

Name

1.

Friends are _____
_____ .

tape and fold

2.

You can do all sorts of things with friends, like
_____ .

tape and fold

3.

Friends help you out in a pinch. One time a friend helped me out by_____
_____ .

tape and fold

fold

4.

The best thing about a friend is _____
_____ .

tape and fold

5.

I like my friends because_____
_____ .

fold

Friendship Word Chain...

Find the friendship words in the chain...

laughugrin

Tell why each goes with friendship!

Write your own friendship chain!

Name _____

Animal friendships...

Write a friendship story about one of these animals. Cut out pages the same shape as the animal and rewrite your story on the pages. Add illustrations! Thinking of a different animal? Draw your own shape!

Plan a friendship Puppet Show...

1. Consider... when might you need a friend?

When might a friend need you?

2. Combine your ideas into a puppet show conversation.

3. Draw yourself and a friend. Cut out the drawings. Tape a straw to the back of each of them.

4. Practice making the puppets talk to each other.

5. Present your puppet show!

Name

Bulletin Board Ideas

Friends Are . . .

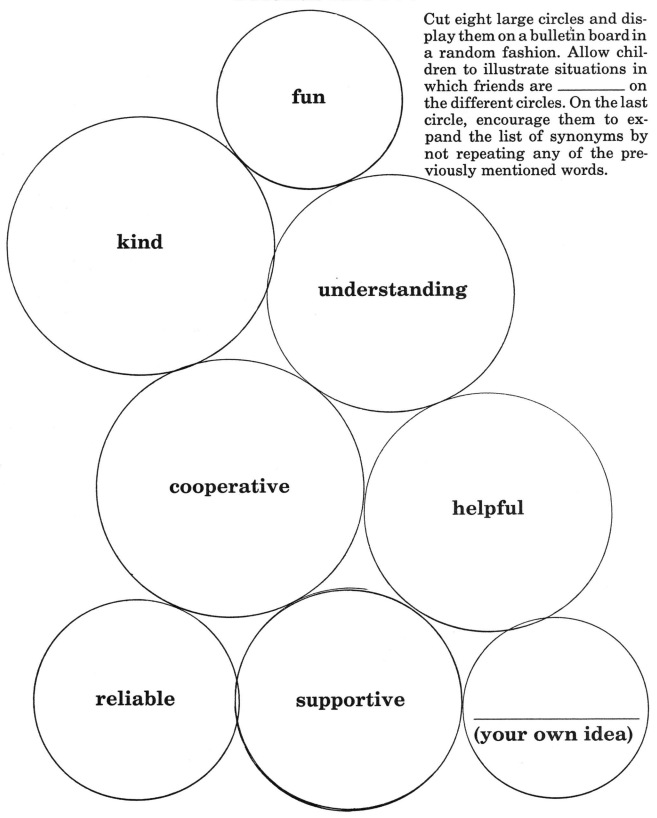

Cut eight large circles and display them on a bulletin board in a random fashion. Allow children to illustrate situations in which friends are _____ on the different circles. On the last circle, encourage them to expand the list of synonyms by not repeating any of the previously mentioned words.

fun

kind

understanding

cooperative

helpful

reliable

supportive

_____
(your own idea)

Friendship Web

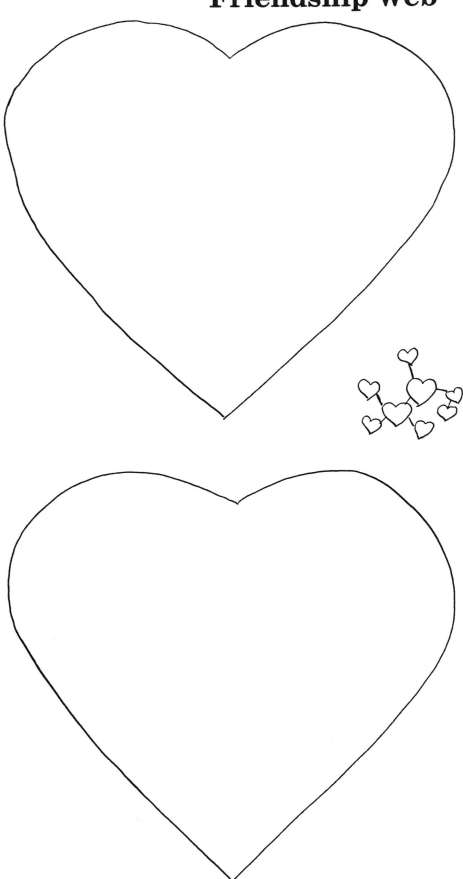

Start a "web" of friendship ideas by having children write on the heart patterns the things they like to do with friends. "Web" them with yarn on a bulletin board. Post a large heart in the middle with the sentence starter—"When I'm with a friend, I like to . . ."

PARENT CONNECTIONS

FRIENDSHIP

Have students find pictures from their family photograph collection of themselves doing something with a friend. Share, compare, and enjoy! Consider taking pictures at school of special friend activities.

Search through newspapers to find examples of friendship—people, animals, and countries.

Collect and display stories about special animal and animal-person friendships (Ex.: Lassie and Timmy, Frog and Toad).

11

St. Patrick's Day

TEACHING ACTIVITIES

A WEE BIT OF CREATIVITY

Fluency
Make a list of all the wee folk similar to leprechauns. Draw pictures of leprechauns, trolls, elves, etc. How are they alike? How are they different?

Flexibility
Put yourself in a leprechaun's shoes. What sort of "training program" is necessary before you can be a successful leprechaun? Think about the skills and secrets of the wee folk. Write a training manual.

Originality
Leprechauns cast their magic by reciting short rhymes. Compose several magical rhymes of your own!
> *Example:*

> Pencils of green,
> Crayons of yellow,
> Make this student
> A very rich fellow!

Elaboration
How can you capture a leprechaun? Model or draw an elaborate trap—one that's sure to catch a leprechaun!

Observation

Survey friends and neighbors. Ask them to tell you three things they know about leprechauns. Tally answers, then write a newspaper story using your results.

SHAMROCK SHENANIGANS

Fluency

What are all the things you can make in the shape of a shamrock? (Example: shamrock pizza, shamrock pencil topper, etc.)

Flexibility

If you were a good luck shamrock . . .

How would it feel?

How would you help the principal? a leprechaun? a pet? your best friend? the President? your grandparents? your favorite make-believe character?

Make a class book. Flip up shamrock shapes to show answers.

Originality

Personalize a shamrock shape to reflect special characteristics of your family (people, hobbies, traditions, special belongings, travels, etc.).

Elaboration

Cut shamrocks of different sizes and different hues of green. Fold them in a variety of ways to cut doily patterns into them. Hang them on a mobile!

Observation

Poll your friends and teachers. If they found a four-leaf clover, what good luck would they hope for?

CLASSIFICATION CHALLENGES

Fluency

Make a long list of words associated with March using the following categories: St. Patrick's Day, weather, plants, and kites. Are there words that can go in several categories? Explain why.

Flexibility

Use the list mentioned above to study word configurations. Which are alike?

Originality

Have class members give informal 3-minute speeches about one of the categories. Can they use all the words in the category in their allotted time?

Elaboration

Draw a picture for each category. Use all the words in your category by labeling your picture.

Observation

Make a word chain using the words from one category.

SYMMETRY

Fluency

Find lots of natural examples of symmetry.

Flexibility

Find examples of things that are *not* symmetrical.

Originality

What if everything were symmetrical? How would our lives be different?

Elaboration

Cut symmetrical coloring book pictures in half. Give one half picture to each student to re-create the missing half.

Observation

Hold a mirror vertically on magazine pictures and photographs to study symmetrical wholes. What do you notice?

GREEN

Fluency

List all the different names for green. Make a color chart.

Flexibility

Have fun with a sentence pattern!
You wouldn't want a _____ to be green because _____ .

Originality

Invent a green character. Write a story about it including as many green things as possible.

Elaboration

Make a collage or mobile of many different green materials.

Observation

Green is a basic color for camouflage. Draw a picture in which everyday objects are camouflaged.

HOW TO USE THE WORKSHEETS

TEACHING SUGGESTIONS

Following are suggestions for using the reproducible worksheets on pages 177–181. These are preceded by a management sheet to help you keep track of children's activities.

Shamrock Decorations (Fluency)

Discuss color and design possibilities before children independently complete this worksheet. As an extension, display their work in a center and encourage individuals to classify the ways the shamrocks are decorated.

Put Yourself in a Leprechaun's Shoes (Flexibility)

Look up stories about leprechauns in the library. Brainstorm different situations in which leprechauns may be involved—role play! Use the worksheet as an independent follow-up.

Leprechaun Lore (Originality)

After children have written stories from these titles, use the stories as a bulletin board border. Or, encourage more stories that stem from their own titles.

St. Patrick's Day Planning (Elaboration)

Involve students in planning their St. Patrick's Day! Organize committees and give children the responsibility for conducting the activities.

Stop, Look, List (Observation)

Have fun with this worksheet on St. Patrick's Day. As an extension, have students create a picture that includes all the things from their fluency list. Duplicate the pictures. Have students color the pictures substituting other colors for the green.

Saint Patrick's Day Management Sheet

Names	Shamrock Decorations	Put Yourself in a Leprechaun's Shoes	Leprechaun Lore	St. Patrick's Day Planning	Stop, Look, List

Shamrock Decorations

How many different ways can you decorate a shamrock?

Name

Extension: Use all the different shamrock designs as a bulletin board ... or use them to invent a code! example: a = 🍀

Put yourself in a leprechaun's shoes...

List all the things you could do to make a leprechaun happy enough to stay at your school.

Name_____

Read several stories about leprechauns. Make your own accordion-fold books.

Leprechaun Lore

✂ cut

The Best Way to Catch a Leprechaun by

Fold

✂ cut

If I Had a Pot of Gold!

Fold

Fold

St. Patrick's Day

Planning

In what ways could your class enjoy St. Patrick's Day all day long?

reading

math

science

Social studies

playtime

writing

lunch

?

Name _____

STOP, LOOK, and LIST!

Observe your world for five minutes.
List all the things that are green!

Now, what if green were eliminated?
What other colors could the things on your
list be?

Name _____

Bulletin Board Ideas

Review With Riddles

Use this pattern for skill or content review.

Cut out two of the above pattern . . . cut a window in the top pattern (leaving one side intact to fold up and down). Glue the two shapes together. Students choose an object or idea from language arts, science, social studies, math, a story, etc. They illustrate it under the flap and write three clues about the hidden object, one on each of the three leaves of the shamrock.

Post shamrocks and challenge other students to solve the riddles.

Add 'Em Up

Enlarge this leprechaun and display him in the middle of a bulletin board. Design articles of clothing to scatter around him and assign point values to the different pieces. Provide a copy of the leprechaun and challenge children to choose items to create a complete outfit. As they dress him, they add up the point values for each article of clothing. How much is their leprechaun's outfit worth?

Suggestions: To ease evaluating, have children work in pairs. Partners' calculations must agree.

Consider using the same idea on a flannel board. Dress and calculate the worth of the leprechaun as a whole group or center activity.

To focus on the problem solving process, consider allowing students to use calculators.

Green Graffiti

A graffiti board is a large sheet of paper on which children record any number of ideas related to a central theme. For St. Patrick's Day, display a long white sheet of paper and provide a large assortment of green writing instruments. Start a list along the border of the sheet of types of greens . . . keep a thesaurus close at hand for this exercise! Challenge children to record any other ideas that come to mind that are related to "green." Encourage them to think flexibly . . . e.g., "green with envy," "green"—inexperienced, etc.

PARENT CONNECTIONS

ST. PATRICK'S DAY

Define fantasy characters (leprechauns, unicorns, wizards, etc.) with your students. Ask children to interview their parents. Do they have a favorite fantasy character? Why? Why not? Graph the information. Extend with stories, drawings, and original fantasy characters.

Round-robin stories! Start a story at school with *one* sentence. Send it home with one child and ask that the family add a paragraph to the story. The child brings it back the next day, and it is sent home with another child the next afternoon. Each family adds to the story. Ask the last family to finish it. Post it on a bulletin board for all to enjoy.

Collect pictures of leprechauns from newspapers and magazines. Classify them. Display pictures on a poster or put pictures on individual cards to make a classification game.

Sponsor a "Green Feast" day! Ask all class members to bring in a special green food to share on a particular day. Invite administrators and specialists to participate. Encourage conversations about likenesses/differences of the offerings.

12

Spring

TEACHING ACTIVITIES

SPRING

Fluency
Do a webbing of spring. Keep going until you have thought of everything you can that is associated with spring!

Flexibility
What are all the different meanings of the word "spring"?

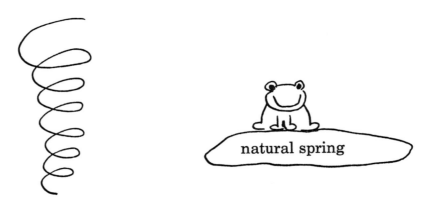

natural spring

mechanical spring

Originality

Create springs from many different materials.

Elaboration

Make a spring mobile using pipe cleaner springs.

Observation

Investigate different springs—draw conclusions.
Collect some different springs. Build a creature from them.

ARBOR DAY

Fluency

How many different kinds of texture rubbings can you get from a tree?

Flexibility

Look at the different shapes of trees. Of what other things do they remind you?

Originality

Make a landscape plan that includes a tree.

Elaboration

Read some poems about trees. Make a recording of your readings.

Observation

Make a mural to show what trees do for animals.

A IS FOR APRIL

Fluency

Make a long list of words that start with "a." Use them to write some *alliterative* sentences. Example: *Archie achieved an A.*

Flexibility

Le_ve _pril fool mess_ges in which you elimin_te _ll the *A*s.

Originality

Design some "April Awards"! (Examples: most blooming look, springiest step)

Elaboration
Create a code using different print styles of *A*s.

Observation
Take note of people's favorite *a*ctivities in *A*pril.

TIME CHANGES

Fluency
What are all the things you would like to do with an extra hour? What adjustments would you make in your day if you lost an hour?

Flexibility
How do animals, plants, buildings, and cars know that time has passed?

Originality
Design clocks for people with different interests—athletes, musicians, etc.

Elaboration
Write elaborate endings to this sentence:

Time has passed when . . . (the seasons change, I get new clothes, our class goes to lunch, etc.).

Observation
Note places and things that mention the time changes (radios, newspapers, football games, etc.). How do they affect different people?

SPRINGS AND THINGS

Fluency
List and collect pictures of all kinds of gadgets.

Flexibility
Use the gadgets to create a cause/effect machine.

Originality
The origin of the word "gadget" is unknown. Write a story that could explain its invention.

Elaboration

List synonyms for gadget (widget, thing-a-ma-bob, doo-dad, etc.). In a demonstration of how to use a particular gadget, use the synonyms when describing the parts of your gadget.

Observation

Classify the gadgets you collected in several different ways.

HOW TO USE THE WORKSHEETS

TEACHING SUGGESTIONS

Following are suggestions for using each of the worksheets on pages 191–195. These are preceded by a management sheet you can use for individual recordkeeping.

Spring Beginnings (Originality)

This worksheet is a good long-term assignment or center activity. Brainstorm possibilities for each box, and have children complete it independently.

March Happenings (Fluency)

Try using the ideas from this worksheet in a class poem on a bulletin board. Or, display the children's poems and provide a graffiti spot for others to add their own thoughts.

A Perfect Spring Day (Elaboration)

Encourage lots of details in a class discussion before using this worksheet. Consider a variety of response forms—pictures, lists, descriptive paragraphs, etc.

Spring Viewpoints (Flexibility)

Role play possible feelings and behaviors plants and animals have as spring approaches. Consider a wide variety of animals/plants. Allow children to create a puppet as a follow-up.

Spring Observations

Model a few examples with the class and allow students a generous period of time in which to complete their observations.

Spring Management Sheet

Names	Spring Beginnings	March Happenings	A Perfect Spring Day	Spring Viewpoints	Spring Observations

Spring Beginnings

Think of some special things to share for spring! Draw an unusual picture, invent a new word and create an intriguing recipe for spring! Tell why each is an original idea.

Spring Recipe

New Word Spring

Spring Picture

Name _____

March Happenings

Complete the sentence below in as many ways as possible. Have a friend proofread it. Copy it onto a poster and illustrate it as a spring poem!

I Know March Is Here When...

_____

_____

_____

_____

_____

_____

_____

_____ Name

The Perfect Spring Day

What would make a perfect spring day?

Describe every detail of it below!

Name _____

Spring Viewpoints

Consider how plants and animals feel as winter is ending and spring is beginning. Choose a plant and animal... draw them and write about their spring feelings!

Plant

Animal

Name

Spring Observations

Make a list of people/things that look or act differently in the spring. Predict how they will continue to change throughout the year.

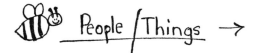 <u>People / Things</u> →   <u>Spring Changes</u>

_____

Name

Bulletin Board Ideas

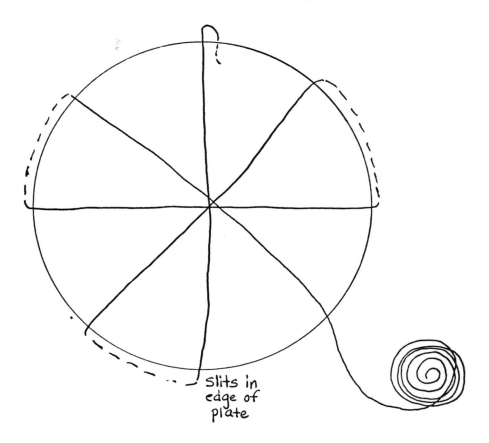

slits in
edge of
plate

Spring String Things

Use paper plates to create colorful "spring string things." Simply notch the edges of a paper plate and provide a variety of yarn for children to weave over the plate in a random fashion. Display some of the children's work from the spring worksheets with the "spring string things" . . . leave extra materials on a table nearby and encourage other classes to join in the spring fun.

Category Compositions

Seasonal Words or Topics	lions lambs	shamrocks	weather
Nouns	livery lawn		
Verbs	laugh	slither shake	
—other skills—			

Post a bulletin board-sized chart that has seasonal words listed across the top and skill areas listed down the side. Challenge children to fill in the boxes with as many alliterative examples as possible that fit the skill category. Then use the chart as a stepping stone to writing stories and sentences . . . or dramatizing some spring merriment!

Example:

The leprechaun at the laundromat laughed at the lopsided load of laundry.

If students are having difficulty filling in a box, and a dictionary isn't helpful, then declare the spot a "free space" for *any* word they might want to write!

Swing Into Spring

As springtime arrives, what plans do students have for enjoying the change in weather? List the ideas for spring activities on a sentence strip border to a bulletin board. Reproduce the above pattern and have students personalize the figure to look like themselves. Use the strips to accordion fold arms and legs and glue them to the body. Cut a rectangular piece of construction paper for a swing seat and suspend it with yarn . . . glue the figure's hands to the yarn so it is positioned as though it is swinging!

PARENT CONNECTIONS

SPRING

Send home a spiral pattern. Have children write on the spiral all the definitions of the word "spring" that they can find. Cut along the lines for a hanging display of springs.

Spy on spring! Ask students to watch their neighborhoods for weather, plant, and animal signs of spring. Designate one bulletin board as a spring graffiti board, and encourage children to record their observations each day.

Send home a morning homework sheet titled "Wake-Up Warm-Ups." List five questions for the week that families could answer during breakfast time. Allow for sharing at school. Sample questions include:

There are seven days in a week. What else comes in sevens?

When is a pie mathematical?

What are all the things you can think of that are white?

What were the first thoughts of family members as they woke up?

What is your favorite winter memory?

How do you prefer to be awakened?

Sponsor a home clean-up! Send home coupons for parents to sign saying how their child helped with cleaning (raking the yard, washing the windows, etc.). As children return the slips to school, keep them in a cleaning bucket. How long does it take to fill the bucket? Add slips for school chores, too. When the bucket is full, have a class "We're All Clean!" party. Play with water balloons, have water relays, and paint on the sidewalk with water.

13

Wind and Kites

TEACHING ACTIVITIES

WIND

Fluency

What are all the ways we notice the wind?

Flexibility

Pronounce wind as wīnd. List words associated with each. Use those words to create a word puzzle.

Originality

List words associated with "wind" (blustery, breeze, etc.). Use as many of your words as possible in a story. Narrate with sound effects.

Elaboration

Show the effects of wind in cartoons or illustrations. Draw objects as they would appear on a still day. Draw the same objects as influenced by the wind.

Observation

What kinds of wind ornaments have you seen (bike streamers, wind chimes, garden whirligigs, etc.)?

BALLOONS

Fluency

How many ways do people use balloons?

Flexibility

Choose a type of balloon. Write a story from the point of view of the balloon.

Originality

Write an original message on a balloon.

Elaboration

Make a character out of balloons.

Observation

List attributes of balloons. What else has each attribute? Make a chart to show your ideas.

FLYING THINGS

Fluency

Make a long list of all the things that fly. Consider powered and unpowered things.

Flexibility

What use do the things from your fluency list have when they cannot fly?

Originality

Combine different parts from objects you listed to design an original flying thing.

Elaboration

Create a mural showing all kinds of flying things. Add unusual details so that the parts create a whole picture and interact with each other.

Observation

In a half-hour period, note all the things that fly by!

PAPER AIRPLANES

Fluency

Explore as many books as possible for information about paper airplanes.

Flexibility

Experiment with tissue paper, cellophane, cardboard, and weights. Does a paper airplane always have to fly?

Originality

Write a ballad or tall tale about a paper airplane.

Elaboration

Make a paper airplane into something else. Add shapes or details to create a flower, a bunny, etc.

Observation

Make observations during a class flight time of student-made airplanes.

Did all paper airplanes fly?

Why do you think some did well and others didn't?

Note flight patterns.

KITES

Fluency

What are all the materials you could use to make a kite? What are all the ways kites could be used in your classroom? Outside? Choose one of your ideas to construct.

Flexibility

What would a bird, an airplane, a cloud, or another kite say to a kite?

Originality

Use library resources to note all the different shapes of kites. What are all the ways you could decorate a kite? Make an original kite. Write the directions for the procedure you followed. Assemble everyone's ideas into a class book.

Elaboration

Write an advertisement for the kite you created.

Observation

Make a timeline of the history of kites. How have they changed over the years? How do they differ depending upon location (beach, mountains, forest, etc.)?

HOW TO USE THE WORKSHEETS

TEACHING SUGGESTIONS

Following are suggestions for using the reproducible worksheets on pages 205-207. These are preceded by a management sheet for use in individual recordkeeping.

Let's Go Fly a Kite (Fluency)

Involve students in planning a kite day, or use this worksheet as a creative thinking activity. Encourage children to bring their own kites to school and start a kite interest center in the classroom.

How Does the World Appear to a Kite? (Flexibility)

Use these worksheet questions for a creative movement activity as children pretend to be a kite. Follow the movement activity with a worksheet writing and sharing time.

Watch People Fly Kites (Observation)

Narrate the flight of a kite as children pantomime an observer's reactions. Focus on the details of facial expressions as students react to what the kite is doing. If available, use mirrors to enable students to study their own expressions. Use the worksheet as follow-up.

Wind and Kites Management Sheet

Names	Let's Go Fly a Kite	How Does the World Appear to a Kite?	Watch People Fly Kites		

Let's go fly a kite!

What are all the materials you could use to make a kite?

What are all the ways kites could be used in your classroom?

What are all the ways kites could be used outside?

Name _____

How does the world appear to a kite...

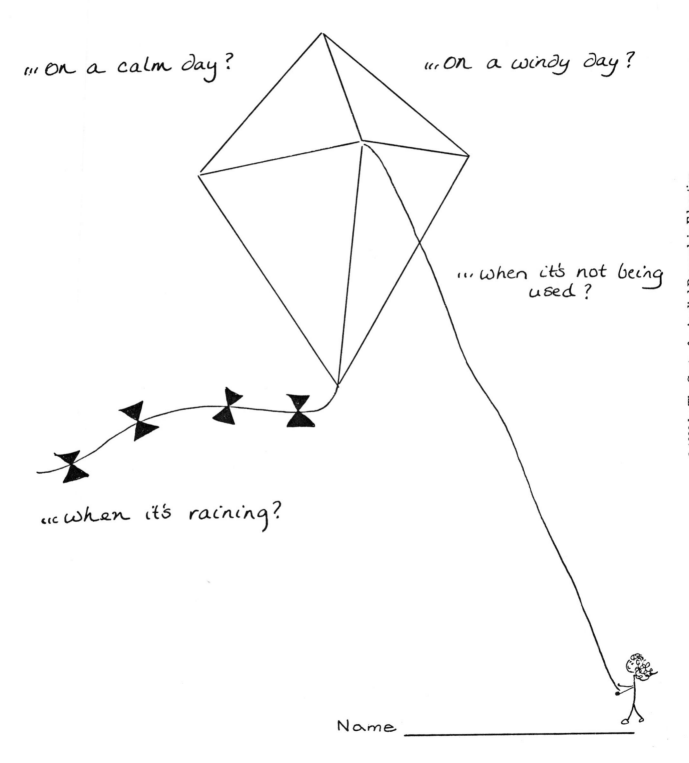

..."on a calm day?

..."on a windy day?

...when it's not being used?

..."when it's raining?

Name _____

Watch!

Draw different expressions people have as they fly their kite and it ...

... gets off the ground.
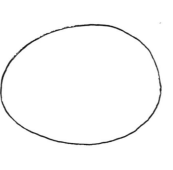

... Swoops.
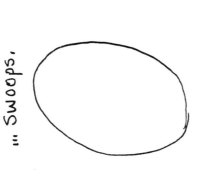

... sails.

... dives.
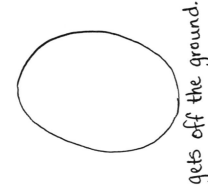

... gets tangled.
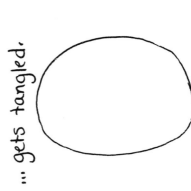

... your choice!

Name _____

Bulletin Board Ideas
Flying Things!

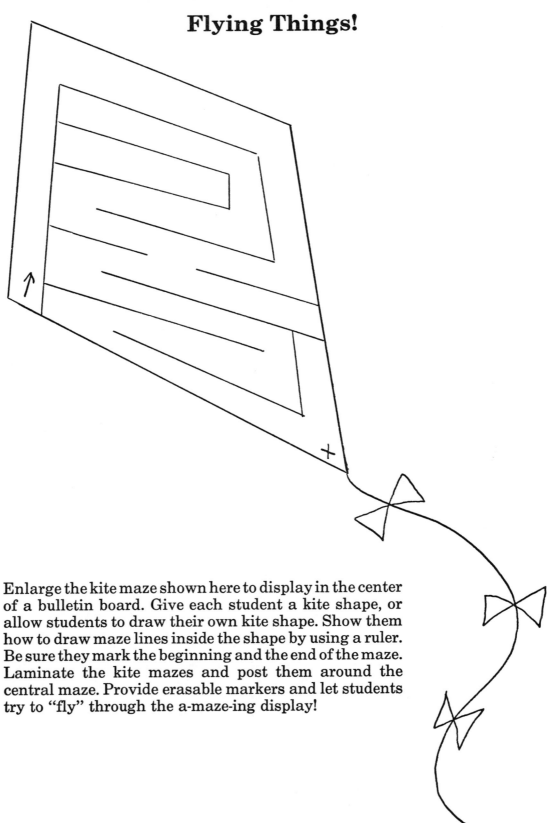

Enlarge the kite maze shown here to display in the center of a bulletin board. Give each student a kite shape, or allow students to draw their own kite shape. Show them how to draw maze lines inside the shape by using a ruler. Be sure they mark the beginning and the end of the maze. Laminate the kite mazes and post them around the central maze. Provide erasable markers and let students try to "fly" through the a-maze-ing display!

Wind Wanderings

Use the following topics as creative writing ideas. Display the children's responses along ribbons that "flow" across the bulletin board.

Did you ever wonder where the wind goes?

Did you ever listen to a wind whisper?

Did you ever hope the wind would push you?

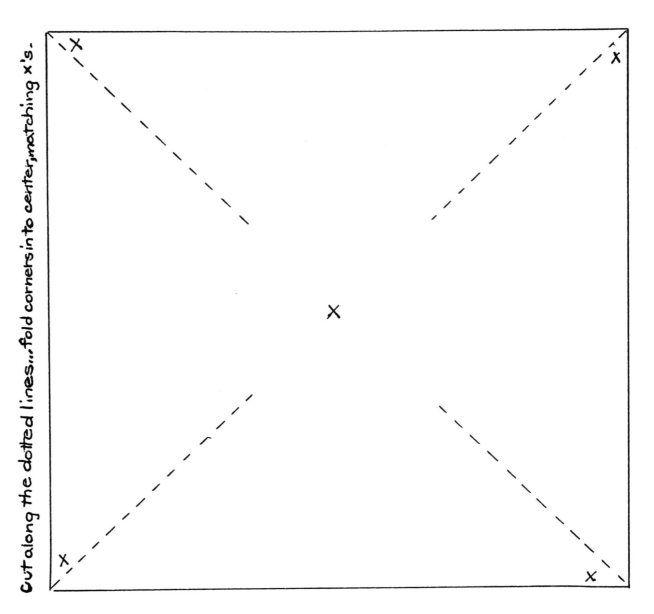

Cut along the dotted lines...fold corners into center, matching x's.

Spin a Story

Create three large bulletin board-sized pinwheels and elicit ideas from children to put on each pinwheel. One pinwheel should list characters, a second should list settings, and the third should list times. Children give each pinwheel a twist . . . and wherever the arrow points is an element they are to weave into a story.

Display the stories around the pinwheels.

PARENT CONNECTIONS

WIND AND KITES

Have students survey their parents to find who has built a model airplane, flown in a hot air balloon, piloted an airplane, etc.

Design a garden or patio whirligig.

Talk about music that makes you think of flying, soaring, or gliding.

Design a paper airplane with Mom and Dad.

14

April Showers

TEACHING ACTIVITIES

PUDDLES WEEK

Fluency
> What are all the things you can think of that would float in a puddle?

Flexibility
> Look up the term "puddle jumper." Make up other terms that include the word "puddle."

Originality
> Write a poem about puddles.

Elaboration
> Go splash in some puddles and then make footprint creatures. Write an elaborate description of your creatures.

Observation
> Notice the reflections in a puddle.

RAINDROPS

Fluency
> Observe throughout the day—what are all the ways that people use water?

Flexibility

Let your imagination go—what else could it rain? (Examples: gumdrops, dog food, pencils, etc.) Compile writings into a class book called "Crazy April Showers."

Originality

Talk about water wheels and the motion of water. Design a water wheel for the year 2000.

Elaboration

Form aluminum foil into a variety of shallow shapes, add water, and freeze to make unusual ice cubes.

Observation

Compare water use at home with water use at school.

Try dropping various liquids (food coloring, perfume, oil, etc.) into a cup of water. What changes occur?

Try dropping various solids (jello cubes, marshmallows, macaroni, etc.) into a cup of water. What changes occur?

APRIL

Fluency

Read! Explore books about rainy days (*Rain* by Peter Spier, *Jemima Puddle Duck* by Beatrix Potter, and nursery rhymes such as "Rain, Rain").

Start a very long list of people and animals that like rain.

Flexibility

Create acrostic sentences using April words.

Example:

Randy

Asks . . .

I

N

Originality

Compose personal reflections of thoughts about rain, storms, puddles, etc.

Elaboration

Investigate facts about rain. Display your findings on a cube or an umbrella shape. Decorate with other things that go along with rain.

Observation

Enjoy a mix of art media! Dust powdered tempera paint on construction paper, carry it out into a sprinkly rain shower, and watch a painting form. Or use watercolor to paint a picture. When dry, sponge or spatter paint on top.

BOOTS

Fluency

On a large strip of bulletin board paper, make prints of every class member's boot soles. To add interest, use different colors of paint. Post all the different things people might say when wearing boots.

Flexibility

Name some uses of boots for when the weather is not rainy.

Originality

Start a fad! Create some boot rhythms or boot tunes!

Elaboration

Boots is a popular name for a dog or a cat. Create a Boots character and describe one of its antics.

Observation

Survey your classmates for different kinds and colors of boots.

SPRINKLES

Fluency

What are all the things you can sprinkle (coconut, fertilizer, water, etc.)?

Flexibility

How do rain sprinkles sound on wood, metal, cardboard, etc.? Try to re-create the sounds.

Originality

People use "sprinkles" on lots of food items. What original sprinkles would you create?

Elaboration

Make a rice mosaic by sprinkling colored rice onto construction paper to form pictures or designs.

Observation

Go outside on a sprinkly day. Count the sprinkles you can catch on a piece of construction paper. When do you lose track?

HOW TO USE THE WORKSHEETS

TEACHING SUGGESTIONS

Following are suggestions for using the reproducible worksheets on pages 217-221. These are preceded by a management sheet for use in individual recordkeeping.

Umbrellas (Fluency)

As children consider a variety of responses to these two umbrella questions, ask for a minimum number of answers to encourage fluency. Compare and contrast answers in a discussion period.

Umbrella Uses (Flexibility)

Use a real umbrella to introduce this worksheet. Encourage students to consider unusual ideas for both an open and closed umbrella. Display responses on the umbrella or a bulletin board.

Magic Umbrella (Elaboration)

Talk about magic and things that have magic with the class. Use this worksheet as independent follow-up. For possible extensions, allow children to dramatize the story, tape record the stories for a listening center, or create a picture to go with the story.

Umbrella Home Project (Observation)

Use this worksheet as a home project. When children return their worksheets, compare and contrast answers in a discussion period. Consider combining the ideas in a variety show that highlights umbrella uses.

Umbrella Advertisement (Originality)

After children have completed this worksheet independently, compile the ideas into an umbrella catalog. Encourage children to share the catalog at home!

April Showers Management Sheet

Names	Umbrellas	Umbrella Uses	Magic Umbrella	Umbrella Home Project	Umbrella Advertisement	

Umbrellas

How many different kinds of umbrellas can you think of?

What are all the things that are shaped like umbrellas?

Name _____

What are all the uses you can think of for an umbrella?

Name_____

If you had a
magic umbrella,
where would
it take you?
What would
happen?

HOME PROJECT

What other things do people use to protect themselves from the weather besides an umbrella?

What are the different ways people carry umbrellas? Take a poll...
Graph the results...
Pantomime them, too!

Umbrella Advertisement

List all the needs that can be met by an umbrella.

Design an umbrella to meet one of those needs.

Write a special advertisement for your umbrella!

Name _____

Bulletin Board Ideas

Sprinkle in Some Numbers

Encourage students to be divergent with math facts . . . post flowers with sums on them and raindrops with addends. How many combinations can the children think of for each flower? Provide record sheets on which children draw the flower they are "solving" and record *all* the number combinations that equal that sum. Students then collect their pages in a "Number Sprinkles" book.

Use this raindrop pattern - or have children draw their own.

Rainy Day Messages

To provide writing reinforcement and spark up rainy days, have children design a "rain boot" and double cut it from construction paper. Post boots on a bulletin board within reach of the students. As a rainy day assignment, have children write messages back and forth using the boots as a mailbox. The "receiver" can edit the message for capital letters and punctuation and then send it back!

As an extension, students can start a rainy day story and "deliver" it to someone else's boot. They add to the story and pass it on to someone else. After a set amount of time, ask everyone to write an ending to their story. Provide time to share the stories.

Paint Puddle Magic

For an unusual spring bulletin board, add white glue to tempera paint and have children create "puddles" on construction paper. When the puddle is dry, students will enjoy feeling the smooth texture and imagining what magic a paint puddle might bring to them. Take time to brainstorm different ideas—the crazier, the better—and then enjoy a writing period. After stories have been edited, display them on a bulletin board next to the puddles.

PARENT CONNECTIONS

APRIL SHOWERS

Make easy weather-watch instruments at school for children to use at home, such as a weather vane, a wind sock, or a rain gauge. As children report their findings back at school, record them on a class record sheet.

Discuss with your family favorite rainy-day activities. At school, compile information in a class book. Make the book available for overnight check-out.

List all the good things about a rainy day. Encourage students to add ideas at later times.

Make a chart to show rainfall in April.

15

Easter

TEACHING ACTIVITIES

CRACK THE CODE

Fluency
Make a very long list of the variety of codes that have been created. Examples include Braille, flags, light flashes, telephone tones, etc. Collect examples for a display.

Flexibility
Create a code for each of the five senses.

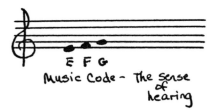

Music Code – The sense of hearing

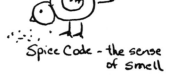

Spice Code – the sense of smell

Originality
Codes often play into mystery stories. Write a story in which a code had to be "cracked" in order to solve the problem.

Elaboration

Read about Samuel F. B. Morse, or another code creator. Write a mini-biography.

Observation

Where are codes used? Why are they used? What occupations use codes every day?

BUNNIES

Fluency

Cut out different pictures of bunnies from the newspaper. Compare them!

Flexibility

Make up a bunny-ear code in which different ear positions indicate different letters.

Originality

Watch a bunny closely. Invent an exercise based upon how a bunny moves!

Elaboration

Brainstorm all the words associated with bunnies. Use them in a story. Write some new verses to "Here Comes Peter Cottontail."

Observation

Make a long list of *famous* bunnies. Compare their individual attributes.

EGGS

Fluency

Make a word search puzzle of compound words that include "egg."

Flexibility

What are all the animals that lay eggs?

Originality

Make up a game using egg cartons.
Create a mosaic using dyed eggshells.

Elaboration

Fix a fancy egg dish for a family meal.

Observation

Share the story "The Goose That Laid the Golden Egg." Interview listeners to find out what they would do if they found a goose that could lay golden eggs.

BASKETS

Fluency

What are all the things you put in baskets?

Flexibility

Research basket-weaving. What materials do you have that would be good for basket-weaving? Consider non-traditional things, too!

Originality

Make a basket for a specific purpose. For example, hang a basket of birdseed on a tree to celebrate Arbor Day.

Elaboration

Think of some famous baskets (Little Red Riding Hood, a tisket—a tasket, etc.). Create a basket mini-museum.

Observation

Compare baskets in your home. Consider size, shape, colors, use, etc. Visit a natural history museum. Note which cultures used baskets.

EASTER PARADE

Fluency

What are all the things you could include in your parade?

Flexibility

Choose an unusual time, type of float, and narration for your parade.

Originality

Choose a theme for your parade. Examples: children's books, spring things, or points of interest in the community.

Elaboration

Design a commemorative set of souvenirs (banners, balloons, cups, hats, etc.) to accompany your parade.

Observation

Write a newspaper story that "covers" your parade!

HOW TO USE THE WORKSHEETS

TEACHING SUGGESTIONS

Following are suggestions for using the reproducible worksheets on pages 231-255. These are preceded by a management sheet for keeping track of children's activities.

Position Available (Elaboration)

Encourage many details as children compose an advertisement for the Easter Bunny's job. Discuss the variety of responses and summarize the ideas into a class advertisement. Assemble students' papers in a shape book.

Egg-stra Special Leftovers (Fluency)

Help parents out with the problem of what to do with left-over Easter eggs by publishing all of the ideas generated from this worksheet. Enlist the help of other classes.

Easter Opinion (Elaboration)

This worksheet could be used as a small group discussion topic, a home project, or an individual assignment. As a possible extension, cut a large class Easter egg shape and have each child illustrate an idea on the egg.

Egg Design Lines (Originality)

After children complete this worksheet, use their eggs as a bulletin board border, an Easter card, a class mobile, a puzzle, a center in which children classify designs, etc. *Hint:* Have children do more than one egg and choose their favorite for the extension activity.

What If . . . (Flexibility)

Consider assigning a different animal to each child to ensure a variety of responses. Or, have a silent response time and extend the activity with a tally of which animals were chosen.

Easter Management Sheet

Names	Position Available	Egg-stra Special Leftovers	Easter Opinions	Egg-Design Lines	What If

Name_____

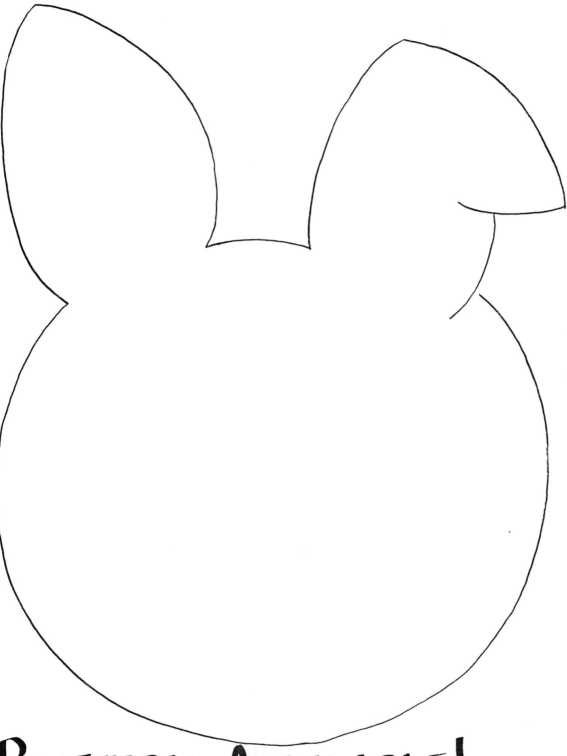

POSITION AVAILABLE!

In the space provided above, write an elaborate advertisement describing the Easter Bunny's job.

Egg-stra Special Leftovers

What are all the uses you can think of for left-over Easter eggs?

Draw or write about them.

✳ **Think** of the egg and its shell.

Name_____

Easter Opinions

Just what egg-xactly would you...

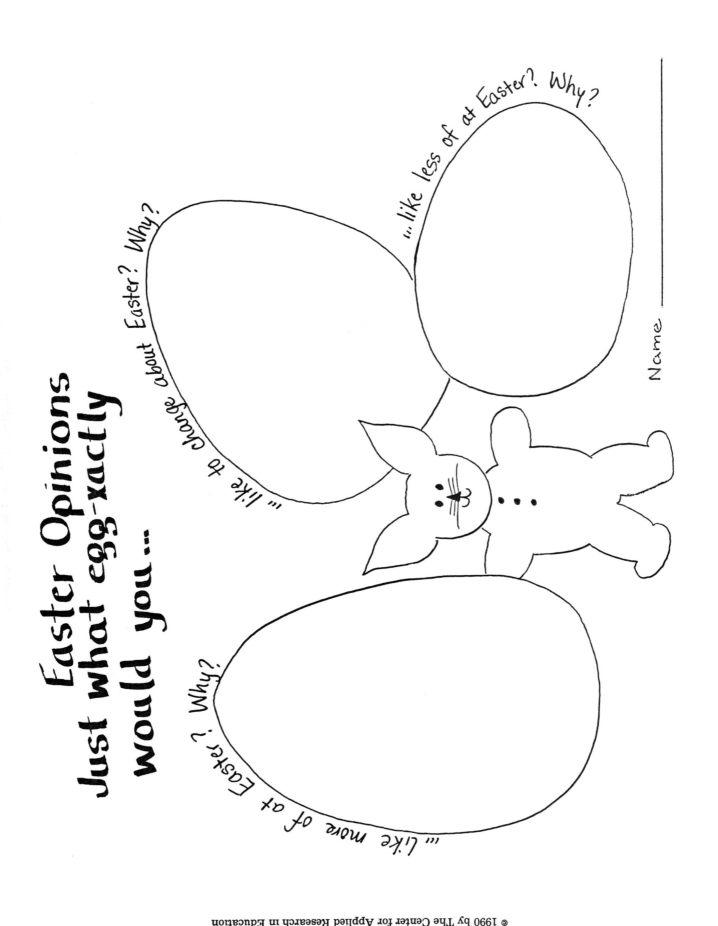

"...like to change about Easter? Why?

"...like less of at Easter? Why?

"...Like more of at Easter? Why?

Name _____

Egg-Design Lines

Draw an Easter egg in the space below. Use a variety of lines and colors to decorate it.

Name _____

What if...

Easter eggs were delivered by .... <u>another</u> animal? Substitute an animal of your choice ... draw and describe your Easter character.

Name _____

Bulletin Board Ideas

Guess What's Inside

Create an interactive bulletin board by having students cut an egg in two, and glue the bottom half to a piece of construction paper while attaching the top half with a brad. Students hide a spring object under the top half, tucked just inside the bottom half so it looks like it's peeping out. They add clues around the border of their paper . . . and others try to guess what's inside the egg.

Observation Puzzle

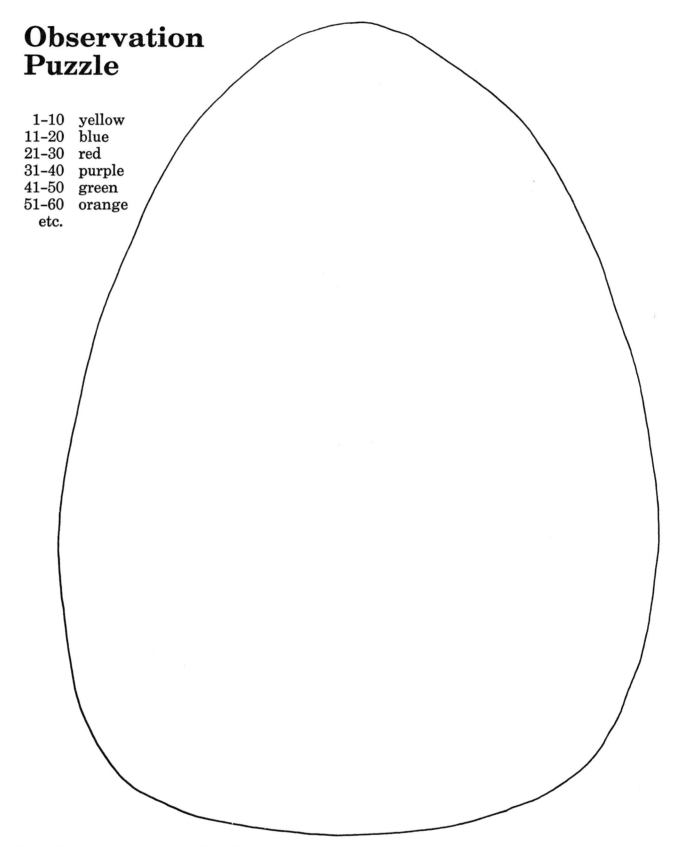

1-10   yellow
11-20 blue
21-30 red
31-40 purple
41-50 green
51-60 orange
  etc.

Provide an egg pattern for all children. Have them criss-cross lines on it to make a patchwork egg. Then ask children to write math problems in each space. Post the code shown aove. Modify the code according to grade level. Children solve their math problems by coloring the space according to the code. Display the patchwork eggs with the code for a divergent math bulletin board!

Hoppin' Along The Bunny Trail . . .

Display the bunny at the bottom of a bulletin board and create a "trail" for the bunny by running a line of cotton balls across the board. Have students paint a picture with a cotton ball dipped in tempera paint. Display paintings along the bunny trail.

Hoppin' Along!

pipe cleaners

black silhouette

cut tail out of white

PARENT CONNECTIONS

EASTER

With your family, substitute words into the song "Easter Parade" to create a song about your family's holiday.

Interview your parents about their memories of special Easter outfits.

Have each family make a poster depicting special family times. Assemble each poster into a Big Book entitled *Family Gatherings.*

Have each student take a plastic egg home to decorate as an animal. As the eggs are returned to school, display them in a large basket. Have students pick one animal from the basket to use as a stimulus to writing a story or elaborate description.

16 ═══════════════════

Sunshine

TEACHING ACTIVITIES

LET CREATIVITY GROW AND GROW

Fluency

How many different flowers can you identify? Collect seed catalogs and make a flower collage from the pictures. Include the name of each flower beside the picture.

Flexibility

Elicit from the class the various places flowers are found. List them in a chart. Have the children take the flowers' points of view and respond in graffiti writing to the question "How do you feel about being in a _____ (forest, garden, ceremony, etc.)?"

Originality

Cut tissue paper shapes of various colors and glue them to construction paper. Collect a variety of objects with which to print flower shapes on top of the tissue paper. Staple the work into a cylinder shape and hang it from the ceiling.

Elaboration

Create a bulletin board by showing before and after pictures of a garden. The left side depicts a garden ready for planting. The right side shows a garden that reflects planning of planting time, types of plants, sunshine needs of plants, etc. (Garden books and information on the back of seed packets are valuable research tools for this activity.)

Observation

Have children spend time collecting strange names of flowers and pictures of those flowers. Display them. Hypothesize explanations of why the flowers might have been so named!

BASK IN BOOKS

Fluency

Start a very long list of books with outdoor settings. Plan to read "outdoor" books *outside* for ten minutes a day. Keep a tally of the total minutes spent with "sunshine reading."

Flexibility

Take different points of view by . . .

- converting a story written in an outdoor setting to a story appropriate for an indoor setting
- choosing a favorite character and composing an original outdoor adventure for that character
- writing from the perspective of the book, i.e., how does it feel to be with children outside?

Originality

Choose a favorite story and create a sunprint bookmark or book cover for it. Cut shapes that are appropriate for the story, lay them on construction paper in a sunny spot, and leave the paper undisturbed until the sun fades the exposed paper. Or, check the local art supply store for special sunprint paper.

Elaboration

Consider a favorite book. Plan a special award designed just for that book. State supporting reasons why the book should receive the award. Conduct a class awards ceremony for the books!

Observation

Consider . . . who would really enjoy some of the books that have been read? Why might that person enjoy them? Write that person a letter telling about the book.

SUNNY IDEAS FOR SUNNY DAYS

Fluency

How many different sunshine "faces" can you design? Put the ideas into a sunshine notepad and send "sunspots" (notes of good news) to your friends.

Flexibility

Use your dictionary to generate a long list of compound "sun" words (e.g., Sunday, sunfish, sundress, or sundrops). Substitute the word "fun" for "sun" so that you have Funday, funglasses, etc. Define each new word and illustrate it in a card that flips open to reveal a picture!

Originality

If you became a sunbeam, how would it feel? What would you look like? How would you change yourself, if given the chance? What's one important thing everyone should know about you?

Bend a coat hanger into a sunshine shape, cover it with tissue paper, add streamers, and print your answers to the questions given above on the different streamers. Display!

Elaboration

Research sun facts. Use them to write a concrete poem.

Observation

Think of all your personal interests. Design a pair of sunglasses that reflect those interests. Fashion them out of construction paper and cellophane.

Take a neighborhood walk and note activities related to sunshine. Substitute your observations into an adapted version of "Old Mac-Donald."

RHYMES WITH MAY

Fluency
List all the things for which you would *say "hurray"!*

Flexibility
Take a piece from all the games you have. Make a new one and *play* it!

Originality
Fray some material. Make a texture collage.

Elaboration
Play with some *clay*. Add details and interesting textures.

Observation
Place objects on a *tray*. Give your partner a thirty-second glimpse. Cover the tray. How many objects can your partner remember?

PATTERNS

Fluency
Collect examples of patterns in nature.

Flexibility
Use examples from above to create a pattern code. Send a message.

Originality
Design some stationery using a pattern.

Elaboration
Compare your daily routine to a pattern. Elaborate by making a chart.

Observation
What patterns do you have in your house or school?

What patterns of events do you have in your family (routines, celebrations, etc.)?

Observe animals for patterns.

HOW TO USE THE WORKSHEETS

TEACHING SUGGESTIONS

Following are suggestions for using the reproducible worksheets on pages 246–250. These are preceded by a management worksheet for individual recordkeeping.

Sunshine Mobile (Originality, Observation)

To facilitate using this worksheet, have the children design the mobile with someone else or something else in mind. What would Mom's mobile show? What would a mobile done by a picnic table show? Provide colored pencils or fine-line markers. Consider cutting out the suns and gluing them on larger pieces of paper.

Sunshine Adventures (Elaboration)

Create a sunflower garden bulletin board by displaying all the books children make using this worksheet.

Sunshine Shopping (Originality)

Encourage children to consider "new" items for use in the sun (e.g., an umbrella that automatically adjusts to keep the sun out of your eyes). As extensions, have children price their items. Provide order forms and practice math skills as they role play shopping.

Favorites (Fluency)

Use this worksheet as an independent activity in which children illustrate their favorite sunshine pastimes. As a follow-up, ask a parent volunteer to guide children in an analysis of why the illustrated activities are favorites.

Sun Substitute

Provide a variety of construction paper and tissue paper (use your scrap box—add both pre-cut shapes and un-cut large pieces) for children to use in completing this worksheet. As an extension, ask children to express the feelings they would have if the sun actually became a different shape or color.

Sunshine Management Sheet

Names	Sunshine Mobile	Sunshine Adventures	Sunshine Shopping	Favorites	Sun Substitute

Sunshine Mobile

What activities do you enjoy in the sun during the different seasons? Draw activities below — cut out the suns. Decorate the back and hang them in a mobile. Add more suns if you'd like!

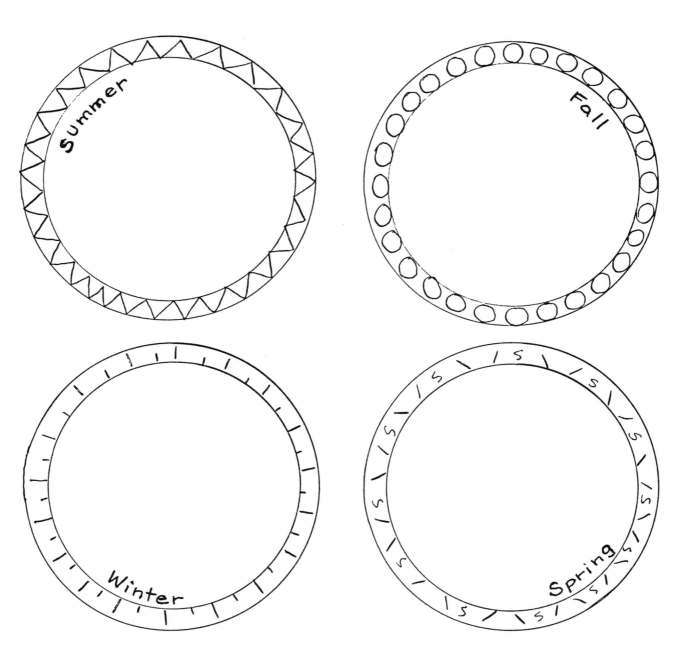

Sunshine Adventures

Choose a main character - write an elaborate
story titled "_____'s Sunshine Adventures."
Rewrite the story on shape pages from the pattern
below - staple into a sunshine book.

Name _____

SUNSHINE SHOPPING

Think of items people use in the sunshine.
Cut along the solid lines below. Fold pages together to
make a sunshine catalogue. Draw and describe items!

✂ cut

Fold and staple

Name:

Fold and staple

Fold and staple

Favorites!

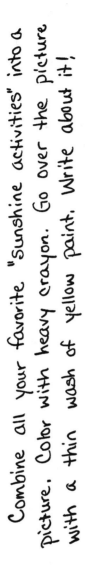

Combine all your favorite "Sunshine activities" into a picture. Color with heavy crayon. Go over the picture with a thin wash of yellow paint. Write about it!

Name _____

Sun Substitute!

Think of different shapes and colors for the sun — combine them in a collage using the space below.

Name _____

Bulletin Board Ideas
Every Minute Matters!

Post these ideas around the sun . . . use them during free time or allow children to substitute them for a daily assignment. As activities are completed, children make a ray for the sun.

- List all the words that are associated with sun (or son!).
- Glue yellow and orange yarn in a sunshine shape on wax paper . . . let it dry and hang it from the ceiling.
- Make a sunshine shaped book of math word problems.
- Write $<$, $>$, $=$, $\neq$ statements about school.
- Draw a picture of "Fun in the Sun" with a buddy illustrator.
- Re-read a basal textbook story.
- Find five things with which to measure . . . measure your desktop with all five. Chart the answers and compare.
- Copy a poem in your best handwriting.
- Monitor a glass of water in the window for temperature change throughout the day. Record on a chart.
- Listen to a record or tape of sunshine songs.

Flowering With Ideas . . .

Name:

Create a bulletin board for May on which children practice fluency and flexibility skills. Make ten large flowers with the following questions posted on their centers:

Name five . . .

reasons why you like May.

things you'll find in student desks.

things you use in the lunchroom.

pieces of playground equipment.

things you know about May flowers.

things you do that make your parents proud.

things you can do with a spoon besides eat.

things to do at a park besides play.

things that a pet needs.

games to play with a friend on a rainy day.

Duplicate this flower worksheet for students to record their responses and post them near the flower with the matching question. After the board is complete, children can compile their pages into a book of their own. Then ask students to add more questions to the board!

Buddies _____ and _____ had fun in the sun!

Let's Have Sun Fun!

Duplicate this sheet for partners to use while sitting outside on a sunny day. Encourage them to draw anything that they agree upon . . . a realistic picture, a picture of themselves, a design, a wish, etc.

Post them on a bulletin board for others to enjoy.

PARENT CONNECTIONS

SUNSHINE

Spring is a beautiful time of year to take a family field trip. Visit nearby historical, educational, amusement, or commercial places. Pick up any interesting maps, brochures, postcards, etc. Organize your material into a poster to share at school.

Spend some time viewing a night-time sky. How many constellations can you locate? Can you discover some new constellations of your own? What kind of folk story would go with your constellation idea? Compose a new "When you wish upon a star" rhyme.

Share a book at home and involve parents in summarizing the story by sending the following letter:

Dear Parents,

Our class has been enjoying reading books in the May sunshine and completing creative products that summarize or extend the story. Please join in the fun by reading this book with your child and completing the attached summary.

Thank you!!

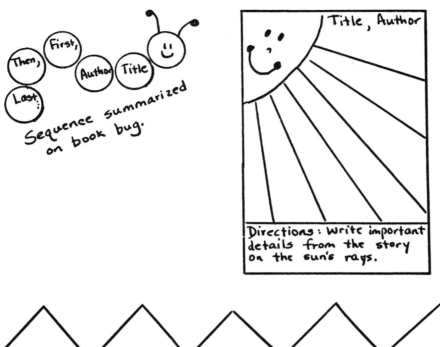

Sequence summarized on book bug.

Title, Author

Directions: Write important details from the story on the sun's rays.

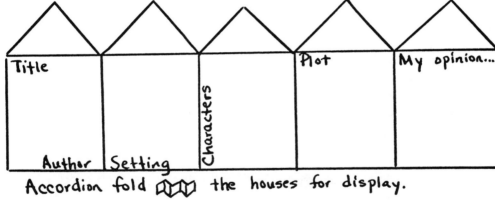

Title

Author Setting Characters Plot My opinion...

Accordion fold the houses for display.

17

Vacations

TEACHING ACTIVITIES

SUMMER SENSATIONS

Fluency

Poll the class to discover what sort of vacation plans students have. Who is going to swim, travel, go to camp, read, take lessons, play outside, learn a craft, start a collection, take on odd jobs, cook, sight-see, play some sports?

Flexibility

Ask for five volunteers to go to the front of the room. Tell them to pretend they have *become* the object they observed (see Observation). Ask the following questions, one by one, of the students. Rotate who answers first. Allow students to pass if they need more time to think. Be sure to return for their answer a little later!

Who are you and what do you look like?

How does it feel to be a _____ ?

If you could change yourself in one way, what would you change? Why?

Suppose your life on earth was about to end . . . What would you do?

Tell us the most important thing you would like everyone to know and remember about you.

Give the rest of the class a chance to respond in writing and allow time for students to read their compositions to a buddy.

Originality

Write a senses poem about the summer.

> In the summer I like to see _____ ,
> I like to hear _____ ,
> I like to smell _____ ,
> I like to touch _____ ,
> I like to taste_____ .

Elaboration

Ask each child to complete a personal planning sheet for summer. Include time frames, modes of transportation, things to do before leaving, benefits, etc.

Observation

After enjoying some time outdoors, call the class together. Direct students to choose some object that they can easily see and to observe only that object for three minutes. Then have them complete an observation sheet (color, shape, size, texture) on that subject.

Once you are back inside the classroom, pose some comparison questions:

How many of you chose objects of the same color? same size? same shape? same texture?

How many are living objects? non-living?

Which are moveable? stationary?

Try showing these relationships in Venn diagrams. List the appropriate objects in the circles that represent them. What other attributes can your students think of to compare?

ahh . . . JUNE!

Fluency

Have students think of lots of different ways to relax. Encourage them to ask parents and friends for ideas. List the ideas on a classroom graffiti board. Plan to incorporate some of the relaxing ideas into the schedule for both the end of the year and next year!

Flexibility

Take a different point of view for end-of-the-year work sessions. Play music softly, vary the working environment, mix group and team efforts in with individual assignments, and coach children in giving a lesson as a student instructor. Consider altering the product of assignments too—combine skills mastered into project ideas, or ask students to create worksheet ideas.

Originality

As a class or in small groups, target a person who deserves a break and invent a Rube Goldberg machine to alleviate his/her stress. Then, plan ways to provide relaxation opportunities for that person.

Elaboration

Ask students to compose a guided imagery exercise to increase relaxation. As a possible follow-up, have them write a story about a very relaxed day.

Observation

Challenge children to watch how animals relax and to note observations in a journal or sketch pad. Role play ways in which animals settle down to a nap, greet each other, walk, etc. Combine some of the movement ideas into a relaxation routine put to music.

CREATIVITY—AS HANDY AS YOUR PENCIL

Fluency

Brainstorm all the things with which to write besides a pencil. Collect them and use them in a class autograph party!

Flexibility

As students consider summer plans, have them "timeline" a plan for using their left-over school supplies.

Originality

Challenge children to write a conversation two school supplies might have about the end of the year—dramatize!

Elaboration

Create an end-of-the-year bulletin board by tracing school supplies right on the backing paper. Have children create imaginary creatures out of them. Add sentences or stories about the drawings. (This strategy makes for easy clean-up on the last day of school. Just rip the backing paper off the bulletin board!)

Observation

Ask your local office supply store for a few sample catalogs. Have children look through them to make two lists—things they currently use and things that would be fun for next year. Consider their ideas in your supply order for next year's class.

As an extension, compare the two lists in cost, purpose, practicality of items, etc. Make it a calculator activity.

CAREFREE CREATIVITY!

Fluency

List all the words your group can think of that relate to sponges. Alphabetize them into a "sponge dictionary."

Flexibility

How many different uses can you think of for sponges? Create some advertisements for your best ideas.

Divide students into small groups and have them create math word problems using sponges as the topic. Write the problems on index cards and have each group trade with another group. Whose problems are harder? Why?

Originality

Use sponges with water to sponge "paint" on the sidewalk. "Paint" in both the shade and the sun. Note the evaporation times for your two creations. Compare . . . what conclusions can you draw?

Sponge paint with tempera paint on newsprint. Write sponge words, create a sponge world . . . think of something spongy!

Elaboration

Write an elaborate story about "The Day the Sponge . . ." or "The Most Famous Sponge."

Create a geometric design using your sponge shapes. Look at all sides of your sponge and cut it if you wish.

Think social studies! Write some rules of etiquette for using sponges.

Observation

Fill a dry sponge with water. Use a measuring cup to see how much water was absorbed. Now fill a wrung-out sponge with water. How much does it absorb? Compare your findings and draw conclusions.

Follow the same procedure, but use a heavier liquid such as dish detergent. What differences do you note?

Note: Other good objects for "Carefree Creativity" are beans, straws, marbles, and toothpicks . . . almost anything that is small, available in quantity, and inexpensive!

JUMP INTO JUNE

Fluency

List synonyms for the word "jump"—incorporate them into a story.

Flexibility

Springs jump! Experiment with a variety of springs. Note patterns of jumping. Attach them to different objects (paper, wood, rock, etc.) and explore "single spring power" vs. "double spring power."

Originality

Paint or chalk a large mural of *everything* that jumps (animals, kids, toys, etc.).

Enjoy a jump rope routine while listening to music.

Elaboration

Practice skip counting as you walk, snap, tap, etc.

Try broad jumping and measuring how far you jump.

Observation

Explore careers that involve jumping (stunt people, athletes, parachutists, etc.).

HOW TO USE THE WORKSHEETS

TEACHING SUGGESTIONS

Following are suggestions for using the reproducible worksheets on pages 263–267. These are preceded by a management sheet for recording students' activities.

Pack Your Bags (Fluency)

Brainstorm types of vacation plans children have, then use the worksheet as a follow-up writing activity. For an extension, set up a reading center with a real suitcase in which to display each student's writing. Add library books about vacation spots for children to enjoy reading.

Vacation Perspectives (Flexibility)

Encourage children to take an alternative point of view as they describe a student's summer vacation, a beach's summer vacation, and a road's summer vacation. Responses may be written, illustrated, or recorded on tape.

Vacation Itinerary (Originality)

Consider having children interview their families before completing this worksheet. Define and discuss itineraries—model planning a trip that suits different interests. For example, if Mom likes painting, Dad likes walking in the woods, and Sue likes swimming, the family plans a trip to the mountains. Provide magazines and materials from a travel agency to use as references.

Dream Vacation (Elaboration)

Use this worksheet as an independent creative thinking assignment. Brainstorm fanciful dream vacations. Encourage children to consider all the details of getting ready for a trip such as laundry, supplies, etc. As an extension activity, have them draw a map of the route to be taken.

Careers 'n Vacations (Observation)

Conduct a class discussion in which children tell about vacations they've enjoyed and what careers (seen and unseen) were necessary for their vacation enjoyment. (Examples: "seen"—an amusement park ride operator, "unseen"—a restaurant cook) Have the children complete the worksheet independently. A challenging extension question would be to ask what careers the children would choose to match their vacation preferences.

Vacations Management Sheet

Names	Pack Your Bags	Vacation Perspectives	Vacation Itinerary	Dream Vacation	Careers 'n Vacations

Name _____

PACK YOUR BAGS

What are all the reasons people look forward to vacations?

What are all the things that could spoil a vacation?

Vacation Perspectives

Describe sumer vacation from the point of view of...

... a student.

... a sandy beach.

... the road to a popular vacation spot.

Name _____

Identify the most important part of a vacation for each member of your family:

VACATION ITINERARY

Now, design a family dream vacation that would include each of these requirements.

Name _____

_____'s Dream Vacation

(Name)

Make an __elaborate__ plan!

My itinerary	My packing list	Things to do before I leave on my trip.

Careers 'n Vacations

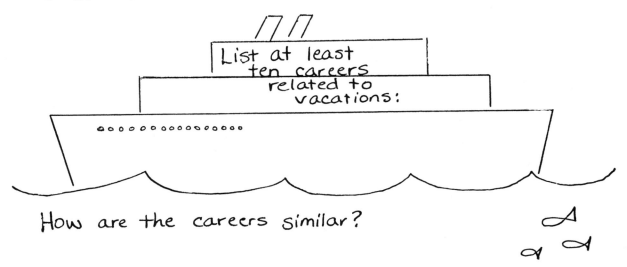

List at least
ten careers
related to
vacations:

How are the careers similar?

How are they different?

Name _____

Bulletin Board Ideas

Unmask Multiple Meanings	A - anchor	C - clipping comic	D° D - degree	E - exercise
G - guide	h - hand	J - jar	K - key	L - line
N - note	B - bear	Q - quarter	R - race	S - scale
F - face	I - iron	free X Space!	car	Z - zip
u - unit	P - panel	O - order	V - view	Y - yard
M - mark		W - walk		
T - tape				

Unmask Multiple Meanings

Use the last month of school to have fun with multiple meanings of words. Post a word a day on a bulletin-board grid, verbally explore the meanings of the word with the class and then ask children to draw pictures, write sentences, act out meanings, create new meanings, etc.

SCURRYING FOR SKILL REVIEW

Go! Enjoy reviewing the skills you've learned this year.

List the table of contents for your math book. Give an example problem for each chapter.

Mary had 5 apples. Sue had 3. How many.....

Paint a picture of things that rhyme.

Write a fact and an opinion about your school helpers.

facts   opinions
1.   1.
2.   2.
3.   3.
4.   4.
5.   5.

Make a shobox museum of your favorite reading book characters.

Write about your favorite Science unit and why you enjoyed it.

Write five directions the class must follow. Tape record them. Have your teacher play them to the class.

1.
2.
3. 4. 5.

Complete the activities independently!

Name: _____

Re-read a book/story shared during the year. Write who, what, when, where and why questions about it.

Make a puppet who loves a particular skill. Examples: "a math puppet," "a vowel puppet"

Design

a poster of your favorite holiday at school.

Draw favorite music activities on large musical notes. Hang the notes in a mobile.

Lead your class in a favorite game or activity from p.e.

Use this bulletin board as a review technique for the skills you've studied this year. As children complete the activities around the board, allow "autographing" the square that corresponds to their work. Or give each child a copy of the game and a folder . . . they collect their work in the folder and color each activity square as they complete it.

PARENT CONNECTIONS

VACATIONS

Why not let June be a time when your classroom becomes more student-directed? Use these ideas to *start* a project . . . then let student ingenuity take over!

Post a large map in your classroom. Have students find out all the places they have visited for vacations and place a pin on the map at those locations. Use the map pins to discuss the popularity of certain places, the reasons for "empty" spaces on the map, criteria for perfect vacations, etc.

Play "Guess Where I Was?" Students show vacation pictures and classmates try to guess the location using visual clues from the photograph or postcard.